THE MARSHALL CAVENDISH
★ ★ ★ ILLUSTRATED ★ ★ ★
ENCYCLOPEDIA OF
WORLD WAR II

VOLUME 21

THE MARSHALL CAVENDISH ☆ ☆ ☆ ILLUSTRATED ☆ ☆ ☆ ENCYCLOPEDIA OF

WORLD WAR II

Based on the original text by
Lieutenant Colonel Eddy Bauer

CONSULTANT EDITOR

Brigadier General James L. Collins, Jr., U.S.A.

CHIEF OF MILITARY HISTORY,
DEPARTMENT OF THE ARMY

MARSHALL CAVENDISH CORPORATION/NEW YORK

CONTENTS

Editorial Director: Brian Innes
Editor-in-chief; Brigadier Peter Young, D.S.O., M.C., M.A.
Managing Editor: Richard Humble
Editor: Christopher Chant
Art Editor: Jim Bridge

As a piece of real estate, Iwo Jima has little to offer anyone: it is an island $4\frac{2}{3}$ miles long and $2\frac{1}{2}$ miles wide at its southern end, dominated by the 550-foot high Mount Suribachi, an extinct volcano. There are some sulphur deposits, a plain of black volcanic sand, and in the north a plateau of ridges and gorges between 340 and 368 feet high. In 1944 there were five villages on the island, in the centre and to the north of the plateau.

The importance of the island to both the Japanese and the Americans lay in the two airfields that had been built, and the third under construction, by the Japanese. From these bases Japanese aircraft could intercept the B-29's bombing Japan, and operate against the bomber bases in the Marianas. The island, if captured, would provide the U.S. with a fighter base and emergency landing strips for crippled bombers.

The island's commander, Lieutenant-General Tadamichi Kuribayashi, was fully aware of the island's importance, and set out a series of "Courageous Battle Vows" for the defenders. One of these was "Above all, we shall dedicate ourselves and our entire strength to the defence of the islands."

Kuribayashi's men worked hard, and by the summer of 1944 had driven tunnels through the plateau, laid minefields, and built gun and machine gun emplacements. U.S. reconnaissance aircraft and submarines located 642 blockhouses before the landings.

Never loath to expend vast amounts of material in an effort to spare the lives of their men, the Americans began early with the bombardment of Iwo Jima. On June 15, 1944, carrier planes struck at the island. The attacks continued during the rest of the year, reaching a climax with continuous strikes for 74 days by Saipan-based bombers. The final three-day naval bombardment was carried out by six battleships and their support elements.

The leading wave of L.V.T.s hit the beach at 0902 hours on February 19, 1945 to the north-east of Mt. Suribachi and began immediately to claw its way up the black sand.

The assault troops were men of the 4th Marine (Major-General Clifton B. Cates) and 5th Marine (Major-General Keller E. Rockey) Divisions, both part of Major-General Harry Schmidt's V 'Phib. Corps. The 3rd Marine Division (Major-General

2803

Iwo Jima

FRONT LINE ON FEBRUARY 19
FRONT LINE ON FEBRUARY 24
FRONT LINE ON MARCH 1
FRONT LINE ON MARCH 11
▲ TAKEN 1020 HOURS ON FEBRUARY 23
⬭ LAST JAPANESE POCKET CEASES TO RESIST ON MARCH 26

Kitano Point

● Nishi

▲ Hill 362

Airfield No. 3 (under construction)

▲ Hill 382

Airfield No. 2

3 Marine Div.

Tachiwa Point

Airfield No. 1

4 Marine Div.

3 Marine Div. (in reserve)

U.S. V Amphibious Corps (Schmidt)

5 Marine Div.

▲ Mt. Suribachi

Tobiishi Point

0   1   2 MILES

Graves B. Erskine) was in corps reserve. In overall command was Lieutenant-General Holland M. Smith.

The troops had practised landings on a similar stretch of beach, and had "stormed" a hill resembling Mount Suribachi. Reconnaissance had also given them some idea of the strength of the defences and the initial bombardment had blown away some of the camouflage and exposed further emplacements. But what they did not know was that their adversaries had built what was probably the most complex defence system in the Pacific. Although only eight square miles in area, Iwo had 800 pillboxes and three miles of tunnels (Kuribayashi had planned 18). Guns were carefully sited to cover the beaches and a series of inland defence lines. The formation entrusted with the defence, the 109th Division, had 13,586 men by February 1, and there were also some 7,347 Navy troops on the island. There were 361 guns of over 75-mm calibre (with 100,000 rounds of ammunition), 300 A.A. guns (150,000 rounds), 20,000 light guns and machine guns (22 million rounds), 130 howitzers (11,700 rounds), 12 heavy mortars (800 rounds), 70 rocket launchers (3,500 rounds), 40 47-mm anti-tank guns (600 rounds), 20 37-mm anti-tank guns (500 rounds), and 22 tanks.

Kuribayashi had elected to fight a static battle inshore from the beaches, but the Navy had insisted that possible landing beaches should be covered by

◁ ◁ *Iwo Jima in February 1945: a small, black volcanic island, dominated from its southern end by Mount Suribachi.*
◁ *Landing craft destroyed by Japanese mortar fire surge against the black sand beach in the Pacific swell. The photograph was taken two days after the initial landings.*

▽ *A Marine, armed with an M1 carbine, covers a patrol slowly working its way up Mount Suribachi. The capture of this important feature was entrusted to the 28th Marine Regiment of Major-General Keller E. Rockey's 5th Marine Division, supported by the 105-mm howitzers of the 3rd Battalion, 13th Marine Regiment, from the same division. Note how good a view of the landings the Japanese would have had. Overleaf: The southern end of Iwo Jima under intensive aerial bombing and naval gunfire attack.*

◁ Marines rest in their
foxholes during the push inland.
▽ American armour makes its
way up to the front past a
knocked-out Japanese gun pit.

▷ A Japanese pillbox, struck
by a direct hit from an amphtrack
armed with a 75-mm howitzer,
blows up.
▽▷ A Marine working party
aids the flow of supplies from an
L.C.I. up to the troops at the
front on March 1.

bunkers. The Japanese tanks were no
match for the American Shermans, and
so were positioned hull down in the
gullies that scored the island. The gun
sites were dug so that the weapon slits
were just visible at ground level, and the
positions were linked with tunnels.

The naval bombardment had driven the
Japanese into their bunkers, and when
the Marines landed, optimists suggested
that it might be an easy operation. Indeed, it is hard to imagine that any of the
defenders could have survived the bombardment, whose finale had included 1,950
rounds of 16-inch shell, 1,500 of 14-inch,
400 of 12-inch, 1,700 of 8-inch, 2,000 of
6-inch, and 31,000 of 5-inch. It was the
heaviest pre-landing bombardment of the
war. In addition to shellfire, the Navy had
also used aircraft to drop bombs and
napalm, and fire a multitude of rockets.
But although some of their weapons were
destroyed, "the Japanese garrison cozily
sat it out in their deep underground
shelters".

The first wave of Marines had crossed
just 200 yards of the beach when they were
caught in a savage cross-fire from hidden
machine guns. Simultaneously, mortars
firing from pits only a few feet wide began
to drop bombs on the men and vessels
along the shore. The U.S. Marine Corps
had embarked on the most costly operation of its history.

Despite the fire from these positions
that needed explosives, flame-throwers

or tanks to overcome, elements of the 5th Marine Division managed to drive across the island on the morning of D-day. When the advance halted for the night at 1800 the Americans were far short of their objectives, but had managed to isolate Mount Suribachi.

Such was the strength of the Japanese positions, however, that it was not until D+3 that the extinct volcano was firmly surrounded. The following morning, the 28th Marines (with the 2nd and 3rd Battalions forward and the 1st in reserve) gained 200 yards of the mountain's lower slopes. The next day an air strike by 40 planes preceded an attack that reached the foot of the mountain. On the 23rd a patrol of the 2nd Battalion's Company F reported that the Japanese had gone to ground. A larger patrol reached the rim of the crater and was involved in a brisk fire fight.

This patrol, under Lieutenant Harold G. Shrier, hoisted a small (54 × 28 inch)

The fighting for Iwo Jima was the bloodiest encountered by the U.S. Marines in their history. But included in the great fleet of supply and support ships that stretched back to the U.S. were hospital ships, fully equipped to deal with all types of combat wounds.

◁ ◁ *A Marine helps a wounded comrade to the beach and transport back to a hospital ship.*
◁ *Support for a 5th Division Marine wounded when a mortar bomb exploded just beside him.*
▽ ◁ *Men of the 28th Marine Regiment, 5th Division, capture the first prisoner to be taken on Iwo. For one and a half days he had feigned death in a shell crater until a Marine saw him breathing faintly. In the centre picture the Japanese is given a cigarette, and in the right-hand one is recovered by stretcher.*
▽ *Three Marines move a wounded man down "Yellow" Beach while under mortar fire.*

▼ The view towards Mount
Suribachi from Motoyama
Airfield No. 1.
► A motorised rocket unit opens
up on a Japanese strongpoint.

The American heavy cruiser *Pensacola*

Displacement: 9,100 tons.
Armament: ten 8-inch, eight 5-inch A.A., two 3-pounder, twenty-four 40-mm, seventeen 20-mm, and eight .5-inch guns, plus four aircraft.
Armour: 3-inch belt, 2-inch deck, $1\frac{1}{2}$-inch turrets and barbettes, and 8-inch control tower.
Speed: $32\frac{1}{2}$ knots.
Length: $585\frac{3}{4}$ feet.
Beam: $65\frac{1}{4}$ feet.
Draught: 22 feet.
Complement: 653 (peace-time).

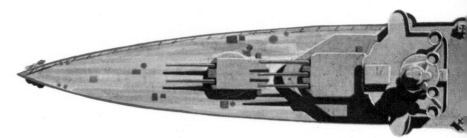

The American destroyer *Allen M. Sumner*

Displacement: 2,200 tons.
Armament: six 5-inch and twelve 40-mm guns, plus ten 21-inch torpedo tubes.
Speed: $36\frac{1}{2}$ knots.
Length: $376\frac{1}{2}$ feet.
Beam: 41 feet.
Draught: 19 feet.
Complement: 350.

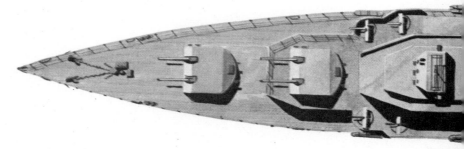

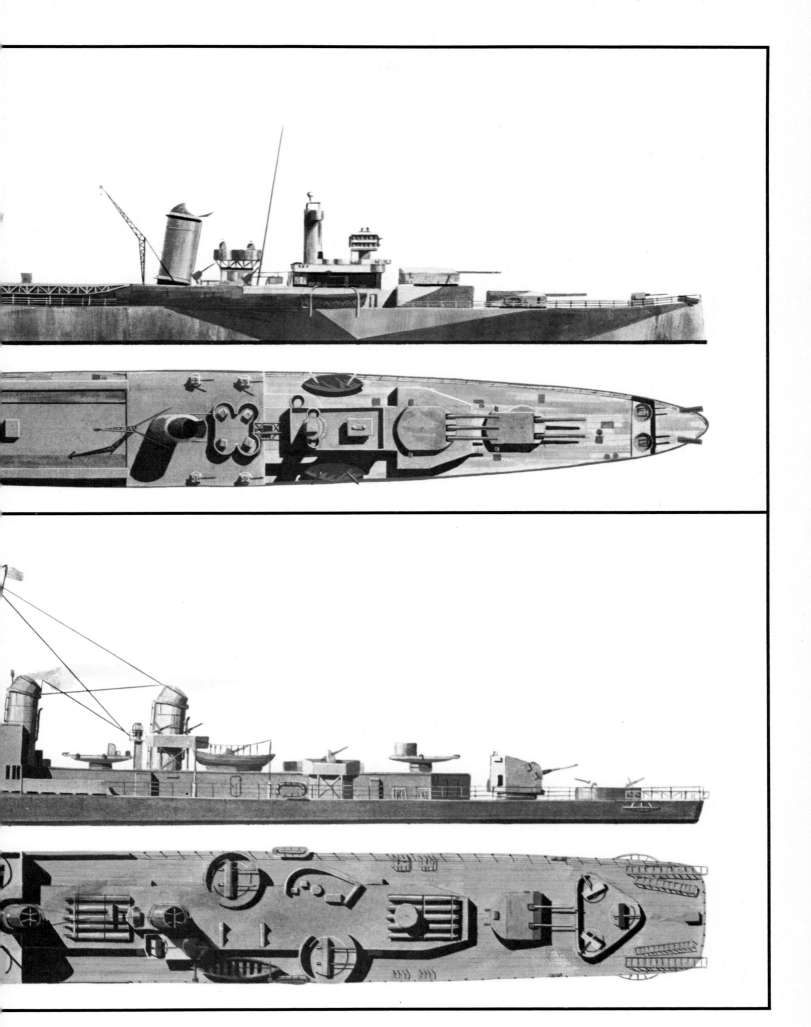

Stars and Stripes flag. Shortly afterwards a larger flag was obtained from an L.S.T., and Schrier decided that this should be raised instead of the first flag. This was photographed by Joe Rosenthal, an Associated Press photographer. The picture of the six men struggling to drive the pole into the volcanic soil has become a classic of the last war.

On March 1, the 28th Marines were moved to the northern sector, to join battalions of the 23rd, 24th, and 25th Marines (4th Division) and the 26th and 27th Marines (5th Division), which had been entrusted with the task of clearing Airfield No. 1 and driving northwards.

It was a battle in which daily gains were measured in hundreds of yards. On February 21 the 21st Marines (3rd Division) were ordered ashore to help.

On the morning of the 24th, after a 76-minute naval bombardment, an air strike, and fire from Marine artillery, the tanks of the 4th and 5th Divisions moved off. One thrust was directed along the western side, and the other along the eastern side, of the airfield. Mines and anti-tank guns stopped the first, but the second pushed on and began to take Japanese emplacements under close range fire. The 5th Division had gained some 500 yards by the end of the day.

On the same day, the 3rd Marine Division landed. and was allotted the task of driving along the centre of Iwo's northern plateau. Once this was taken, the Marines would be able to push down the spurs leading to the sea. The plateau was an extraordinary feature, eroded into fantastic shapes by wind, rain, and volcanic activity.

The division launched its attack at 0930 on the 25th. It was a slow and costly operation, as the attack met the main Japanese line of defences. Three days of attacks, in which the Marines brought up flame-throwing tanks to incinerate the Japanese in their shell-proof bunkers, finally broke through the line. On the 28th the Marines secured the ruins of Motoyama village and the hills overlooking Airfield No. 3. The Americans now held all three airfields, the objectives of the landings, but the fighting was by no means over.

On the last day of the month, the Marines attacked the two small features of Hills 382 and 362A. Their size was misleading, for each contained a warren of tunnels and bunkers. The crest of Hill 382 had been hollowed out and turned

◁ ◁ *Marines burn their way through the outer defences of Mount Suribachi with what the original caption on the photograph describes as "Devil's breath on Hell's island". On the left is Private Richard Klatt of North Fond du Lac, Wisconsin, and on the right Private First Class Wilfred Voegeli.*
▽ ◁ *A captain of the 21st Marine Regiment, 3rd Marine Division, inspects a Japanese dug-out after it has been hit by a bomb.*

◁ *Marines shelter by the remnants of a Japanese sulphur mine and refinery.*
▽ *A 155-mm howitzer blasts away at one of the last Japanese positions in the north of the island.*

into a huge bunker housing anti-tank guns and other artillery. Tanks were sited in the gullies. To the south of the hill there was a massive rock which became known as Turkey Knob, with a natural bowl christened the Amphitheater. The fighting for both features became so intense that they became known as the Meatgrinder. A series of savage local battles was fought on March 1. And although Hill 382 fell that day, it was not until the 10th that the Japanese defending Turkey Knob and the Amphitheater were destroyed.

The attack on the Hill 362A complex on March 2 was a marked departure from normal Marine practice–they attacked at night. Although movement through the rugged terrain was slow and tiring, the tactics surprised the enemy. After a fierce fight on the 8th, the Marines were in possession of the whole area.

Despite the loss of these key points, the Japanese continued to fight with their customary aggressiveness. On the 8th

they launched an attack on the junction between the 23rd and 24th Marines. Caught in the open without artillery support, the attack failed with 650 dead. With this defeat the Japanese defence began to crumble, and the battle moved into the mopping up stage. Individual strongpoints were in no mood to surrender, however, and as they had ample stocks of food, water, and ammunition, they could hold out for some time. Indeed, on March 15, many of the last defenders attempted to infiltrate the American lines.

The last pocket to be destroyed was that at Kitano Point, which was declared officially secure on March 25. But that night over 200 Japanese emerged from the flame-blackened and shell-scarred rocks. Led in person by Kuribayashi, some say, they tore into the bivouac area occupied by the sleeping men of the 5th Pioneer Battalion. A defensive line was set up by the Army's VII Fighter Command and the Marines' 8th Field Depot and by dawn at least 223 Japanese, including their leader, lay dead.

The conquest of Iwo Jima had cost the Marines 5,931 dead and 17,372 wounded. But by the end of the war the island's airfields had saved the lives of 24,761 American pilots and aircrew. Of the 21,000 Japanese defending the island, only 216 were taken prisoner. If this was the cost of taking an island of only eight square miles and which had been Japanese only since 1891, what would be the cost of the conquest of Japan?

▽ *The Americans consolidate: telephone lines fan out from a headquarters north of Mount Suribachi to improve communications between commanders and front line forces mopping up Japanese resistance.*

CHAPTER 169
Okinawa: the plans

Operation "Iceberg" was the name of the plan; the island of Okinawa was the target. The American aim was to achieve the penultimate victory of the Pacific war: the seizure of a firm base on the very doorstep of Japan as a prelude to the final conquest of the Japanese home islands. And the ensuing battle was fought on a scale as yet unknown in the course of the Pacific war: a bloody, protracted fight to the finish which forced the Americans to exert every ounce of their strength. After all the agonising first-hand experience gained in the long road from Guadalcanal to Iwo Jima, Okinawa proved yet again that the Japanese will to resist defied all possible estimates when tested on the battlefield.

The Okinawa plan was given its official blessing by the Joint Chiefs-of-Staff on October 3, 1944. It was envisaged as

only one of three major offensives intended to stretch Japanese resources to their limits, the other two being the conquest of Luzon and the reduction of Iwo Jima in the Bonin Islands. Luzon would be invaded in December 1944, Iwo Jima in January 1945, and Okinawa in March.

In view of the vital nature of the target — a major bastion of Japan's inner island defences – it was essential that as much Intelligence as possible should be amassed. Aerial photography was an obvious source, but the difficulties were considerable. Okinawa was 1,200 miles from the nearest American air bases when it was selected as the objective of "Iceberg". B-29's flying at their high altitude only obtained small-scale photographs; carrier aircraft could only be assigned to Okinawa for photographic reconnaissance when the

◁ ◁ *The celebrated flag raising on Mount Suribachi on February 23. The men raising the pole are, from left to right, Private First Class Ira H. Hayes of Sacaton, Arizona, Private First Class Franklin R. Sousley of Dayton, Ohio, Sergeant Michael Strank of Franklin Borough, Pennsylvania, Pharmacist's Mate 2nd Class John H. Bradley of Appleton, Wisconsin, Private First Class Rene A. Gagnon of Manchester, New Hampshire, and Corporal Harlon H. Block of Yorktown, Texas.*
△ ◁ *Front line communion from Father Joseph Hammond.*
△ *Marines of the 2nd Battalion, 6th Marine Regiment, on "Green" Beach 1 during the Okinawa landings on April 1, 1945. "Green" Beach 1 was the extreme northern flank of the landings.*

△ *Japanese installations and shipping under attack from U.S. carrier-borne aircraft during the preliminary operations for the capture of Okinawa.*
◁ *Flame-thrower tank in action en route to Naha, capital of Okinawa.*

programme of carrier operations permitted. Other problems included the prevalence of local cloud cover and the large size of Okinawa itself: 60 miles long and from 2 to 18 miles wide, making it extremely difficult to obtain a mosaic of photographs covering the whole island. However, reconnaissance did collect sufficient information to suggest that the main strength of the Japanese defences would be encountered in the southern half of the island around Naha and Yontan—the best two out of the four operational airfields on Okinawa. The final estimate of the strength of the garrison was 65,000 men.

Japanese strength

What the cameras failed to reveal was that Lieutenant-General Mitsuru Ushijima's 32nd Army was in fact over 100,000 strong. Regular troops (infantrymen, gunners, and special services) totalled 77,199, and there were 20,000 auxiliary troops known as *Boeitai*. These were drafted into the Japanese Army to serve in labour and supply duties, relieving the fighting troops of ammunition worries, and thus playing an important part in the battle. In addition to the *Boeitai* there was a large contingent of Okinawan conscripts assimilated by the regular units on the island. Precise figures for these conscripts are not available but have been set as high as one-third of the total garrison strength.

Japanese hopes for the defence of Okinawa were strikingly similar to those for the defence of Luzon. The high command ordered that the island must be held. Wildly exaggerated estimates were pinned on the hitting power of the air and sea *kamikaze* forces. It was expected that *kamikaze* attacks on the American invasion fleet and the initial beach-head would cut off the first troops ashore from their supports, making it possible for the Japanese garrison to sally out against the stranded American troops and fling them back into the sea. Like Yamashita on Luzon, however, Ushijima knew how heavily the odds were stacked against him. He had no illusions about what was coming and accepted that he would be unable to stop the Americans from getting ashore and establishing a beach-head too strong to be destroyed.

Ushijima therefore planned to hold the strategically vital southern half of the island with the bulk of the 32nd Army, digging it in and forcing the Americans to batter away at its positions at as high a cost as the Japanese troops could exact. Naha and Shuri were the central nodes of the defence. No landing north of Chaton on the west coast or Taguchi on the east coast (just south of Kadena airfield) would be opposed. The Americans might get ashore. They might overrun the spindly northern region of the island. But until they had destroyed every last stronghold held by the units of the 32nd Army in the south they could not force a decisive victory—let alone claim the conquest of Okinawa and move on to more deadly operations against the Japanese homeland.

The American forces earmarked for the conquest of Okinawa constituted an awesome armada of battle-wise fighting units.

▽ *Plumes of smoke rise from the town of Toguchi on the Motobu peninsula and from the islet of Sesoka after a raid by U.S. strike aircraft.*

△ Marines watch from the crest
of a hill as a barrage of
phosphorus shells explodes on a
Japanese position further down
the slope.
◁ A Marine machine gun crew
provides covering fire.
△▷ A roadside aid station,
manned by naval corpsmen.
From here the seriously wounded
could be sent to the rear after
initial treatment had been given.
The main casualty centre was
warned of the arrival of the more
serious cases by walkie-talkie
radio.
▷ A 37-mm gun of the 6th
Marine Division pounds a
Japanese strongpoint.

△ *American infantry wait for the barrage to lift before continuing their advance.*
△ ▷ *A combined flame-thrower and tank team flushes out a Japanese pocket.*
▷ ▷ *Senior American commanders on Okinawa watch the progress of their plans. From left to right they are Lieutenant-General Simon Bolivar Buckner, commanding general of the 10th Army, Major-General Lemuel C. Shepherd, commanding general of the 6th Marine Division, and Brigadier-General William T. Clement, assistant commander of the division.*
Page 2828: *In the ruins of Naha.*

Responsibility for taking the troops to their target and shielding and supporting them once they came ashore rested with Admiral Raymond A. Spruance's 5th Fleet. Its Joint Expeditionary Force, commanded by Admiral Richmond K. Turner, was designated Task Force 51.

The American invasion fleet

This, the invasion fleet proper, comprised half a million servicemen, over 300 warships, and over 1,139 auxiliary vessels and landing craft. It was shielded by Vice-Admiral Marc A. Mitscher's Task Force 58, which would also carry out the initial bombardment and neutralisation of the Japanese defences. Task Force 58 consisted of four fast carrier groups, together with the British carrier force

commanded by Vice-Admiral Sir Bernard Rawlings, designated Task Force 57 although it was only the equivalent of a single American carrier group.

The land forces consisted of the newly-formed 10th Army under General Simon B. Buckner. Okinawa would be the first battle for 10th Army but not for its component units, as the following breakdown shows:

1. XIV Corps (Major-General John B. Hodge)
7th Infantry Division – Attu, Kwajalein, Leyte
96th Infantry Division – Leyte
2. III Amphibious (Marine) Corps (Major-General Roy S. Geiger)
1st Marine Division – Guadalcanal, New Britain, Peleliu
6th Marine Division – regiments from Marshalls, Guam, Saipan
3. Reserve
27th Infantry Division – Gilberts, Marshalls, Saipan

77th Infantry Division – Guam, Leyte
2nd Marine Division – Guadalcanal, Tarawa, Saipan, Tinian.

Thus the seven divisions which would land on Okinawa were made up of officers and men steeped in the overall experiences and lessons of the Pacific was since August 1942. They totalled about 154,000 men – 116,000 of them belonging to the five divisions which would make the initial landings along the eight-mile sweep of the Hagushi beaches on the west coast between Sunabe and Zampa Point. D-day for Okinawa was set for the morning of April 1, 1945. It was to be preceded by the capture of the Kerama Retto, a group of small islands 20 miles west of southern Okinawa, which would then be used as an advanced base. Diversionary landings would be made on the far side of Okinawa from the Hagushi beaches; if necessary these landings could be reinforced to confront the Japanese with a double beach-head.

CHAPTER 170

Okinawa: the battle

Mitscher's big carriers began the first phase of the softening-up process on March 18, launching heavy strikes against Japanese airfields on Kyūshū. On the 19th the Americans switched to the naval bases at Kobe, Kure, and Hiroshima and to Japanese shipping in the Inland Sea. *Kamikazes* and bombers hit back fiercely, damaging *Yorktown, Wasp,* and *Enterprise* and setting *Franklin* ablaze. Task Force 58 began to withdraw on the afternoon of the 19th, and during the next 48 hours was harried by repeated Japanese air attacks. These, however, were fought off by the American fighter pilots, who ran up impressive scores. The tally of Japanese aircraft destroyed between March 18 and 22 was 528, and 16 surface ships were damaged during the same period, including the super-battleship *Yamato.* Mitscher's force had amply fulfilled its rôle. When the main landings went in on Okinawa, the Japanese were unable to throw in a serious air counter-

attack for a week.

Next on the schedule was the seizure of the islands of the Kerama Retto group, a task entrusted to the 77th Division under Major-General Andrew D. Bruce. This was a campaign within a campaign, a faithful miniature of the "island-hopping" programme as a whole. A preliminary reconnaissance and bombardment preceded the actual assault, which was launched on the islands of Aka, Geruma, Hokaji, and Zanami on March 26. Initial progress was so rapid that Bruce decided to take Yakabi Island as well, and it fell with minimal resistance on the first day. The Japanese reacted in familiar fashion on Aka and Zanami, pulling back into the interior after conceding the fight for the beaches. The same thing happened the following day when Tokashiki was attacked, together with Amuro and Kuba. The Keramas were declared secure on the 29th, but the Japanese on Aka and Toka-shiki insisted on refusing to surrender

Previous page: The face of defeat – a Japanese naval lieutenant surrenders. Before Okinawa, American forces captured various small islands in the area.
Δ▷ *Raising the flag on Aka.*
▽ *Assembling above the beach on Geruma. March 25, 1945.*

until the official capitulation of Japan. The occupation of the Keramas was rounded out with the emplacement of two batteries of 155-mm guns on the coral islands of Keise Shima, a mere 11 miles off the Haguchi beaches. These guns would add to the fire-power of the pre-invasion bombardment, and their emplacement on Keise Shima was a repetition of a trick used with great success during the battle for Kwajalein.

Pre-landing bombardment

While the Keramas were still being cleared, the intricate work of preliminary bombardment and minesweeping in the approaches to Okinawa had already been started by Vice-Admiral William H. Blandy's Task Force 52. The first offshore shelling began on March 25, but the job of clearing the dense minefield which the Japanese had laid off the Hagushi beaches was not completed until the evening of the 29th. Blandy himself called it "probably the largest assault sweep operation ever executed". In the week before the assault the American warships pounded the Japanese defences with over 13,000 shells of calibres ranging from 6-inch to 16-inch, while the carrier planes flew 3,095 sorties, covering targets requested by 10th Army. In the last three days, as the offshore obstacles were cleared, the warships steadily shortened the range and intensified their fire. With the method born of experience and the most detailed planning, an intricate naval ballet man-oeuvred 1,300 ships into position for the assault on the morning of April 1.

"Land the landing force"

Admiral Turner's order was signalled to the invasion fleet at 0406 hours on the 1st—four and a half hours before the moment scheduled for hitting the beaches with the first wave. As the long ranks of

landing-craft jockeyed into position for the approach, the terrain behind the beaches shuddered and smoked like a volcano under the shellfire of the bombardment force. The boats moved off at 0800 in perfect conditions and the run-in proceeded as easily as a peace-time manoeuvre. As the bombardment lifted and the gunfire shifted inland the first boats began to ground, almost exactly on schedule, just after 0830. To the troops the actual landing came as an almost ludicrous anti-climax. "Where are the Japs?" was the question every man was asking as the cautious advance into the interior began. Meanwhile the landings continued without a hitch. By the evening of April 1 over 60,000 troops had landed on Okinawa and had pegged out a beach-head over eight miles wide and over two miles deep in places.

"An enemy landing attempt on the eastern coast of Okinawa on Sunday morning was completely foiled, with heavy losses to the enemy." That was how the Japanese boasted of the feint attack made by 2nd Marine Division (Major-General Thomas E. Watson) on the far side of the island from the Hagushi beaches. The Marines had made it look like a genuine attempt, with eight waves of boats dressed in line and covered by bombardment. They moved in simultaneously with the approach to the Hagushi beaches, reversed course precisely at 0830, and headed back to their parent vessels. The same performance was made on the morning of the 2nd and the force was then withdrawn.

Fast progress

On the second and third days the Marines and infantry pushed right across the island and cut it in two, with 96th and 7th Divisions wheeling to the south on the right flank and feeling out the first serious Japanese resistance around Momabaru. By the evening of April 3 interrogated Japanese civilians and liberated P.O.W.s had informed the advancing troops that the main Japanese forces had pulled back to the south. The puzzle of the non-existent enemy had been solved: the battle for Okinawa had still to begin.

The push to the south was carried out by XXIV Corps: 96th and 7th Divisions, who began the cautious probing of Ushijima's defence outposts. For both divi-sions, April 5 marked the first day when genuine resistance at last was encountered. The advance continued during the next three days but by April 9 both divisions had been fought to a halt and XXIV Corps had not attained its prescribed objective. On the 9th the 383rd Infantry fought its way on to Kakazu Ridge but were forced to withdraw after a bloody fight. A "powerhouse attack" on April 10 was also repulsed, and the Japanese were still very much in possession of their strongpoint at Kakazu on the 12th. The first round had undoubtedly gone to the Japanese in precisely the sort of battle that Ushijima had planned. American morale was also depressed by President Roosevelt's death, which the Japanese promptly exploited for propaganda. "We must express our deep regret over the death of President Roosevelt," ran one leaflet. "The 'American Tragedy' is now raised here at Okinawa with his death .. Not only the late President but anyone else would die in the excess of worry to hear such an annihilative damage. The dreadful loss that led your late leader to death will make you orphans on this island. The Japanese special assault corps will sink your vessels to the last destroyer. You will witness it realised in the near future."

In the overview the Japanese were whistling in the dark: they certainly had little to boast about as far as naval victories were concerned. On April 7 the "Special Sea Attack Force" had sortied on a one-way mission to Okinawa. It was a suicide run, aimed at sending the super-battleship *Yamato* into the midst of the American invasion fleet and dealing out as much destruction as possible before meeting her inevitable end. But *Yamato* had been sunk by carrier planes before she had even sighted Okinawa. With the grip of the American navy unshaken, it was the Japanese who remained the "orphans of Okinawa", for all the local successes they might win. Much more important was the nature of the battle itself, with the Japanese having to accept the consequences of their defensive strategy. The cost of halting XXIV Corps by April 12 had been grievous: about 5,570 for the Japanese and 451 for the Americans. Despite this twelve-fold imbalance, 32nd Army now went over to the offensive to try to exploit the discomfiture of XXIV Corps by pushing it back to the north.

In two days of intense fighting the Japanese counter-attack, carried out by

△ Men of a U.S.A.A.F. liaison squadron rescue one of their Stinson L-5 Sentinels caught in a flash flood on Okinawa. These small planes were invaluable for co-ordinating movements with ground troops.

omponents of 62nd and 24th Divisions, was repelled at all points. It was a costly eviation from the basic strategy of taying in strongpoints and letting the Americans suffer the losses. By dawn on he 14th stalemate had settled once again ver the front line.

Meanwhile Buckner had reversed the riginal plan of tackling southern Okinwa before clearing the north of the sland, and had unleashed Geiger's Marines (6th Marine Division) on April 3. Driving north-eastwards along the nar-

to press ahead with the capture of Ie shima, the 5-mile-long oval island 3½ miles off the Motobu Peninsula. The Japanese had built three airstrips on Ie shima and that was Buckner's main objective: to seize the island and use it as a natural aircraft-carrier to intensify the air umbrella over the Okinawa battlefield. Ie shima was a formidable nut to crack. The 2,000 troops on the island had, by exploiting civilian labour, made it a miniature Iwo Jima as far as prepared defence positions were concerned. Major-General Andrew D.

row "neck" of Okinawa, the 6th Marines had reached the sea and cut off the Motobu Peninsula by April 8. But it took them another 12 days to clear the peninsula and they had to exert every effort to crush the main Japanese position at Yae-Take with concentric attacks. Not until the 20th was Japanese resistance in the peninsula broken, and enough Japanese escaped to the hills to begin organised guerrilla warfare.

After changing his plan and clearing northern Okinawa, Buckner also decided

Bruce's 77th Division was earmarked for the capture of Ie shima, and the landings went in on April 16. Despite vigorous resistance, the 77th Division had overrun the western half of the island with its airstrips by the end of the 16th. But the Japanese still held out in Ie town. Five more gruelling days were needed before the island was declared secure, and even then the fighting continued until the 24th. The fight of Ie shima epitomised the bitterness of the Okinawa campaign; commenting on it, General Bruce said that "the last three days of this fighting were the bitterest I ever witnessed".

Surprise attack

Back on the southern front, Buckner was preparing to succeed with stealth where open attacks had failed: a surprise attack on the Shuri defences, pushing yard." The attack of April 19 was a complete failure and cost XXIV Corps 720 casualties. The Japanese fought like furies and held off all the American attempts to slip round their strongpoints. The zones of fire of their artillery and mortars had been carefully drawn and covered all sectors of the front. One regimental commander in the 96th Division commented bitterly after the battle: "You cannot bypass a Jap because a Jap

deep into the Japanese lines and by-passing strongpoints such as the Kakazu Ridge. The attack was set for April 19 and was to be launched by a surprise penetration by General Hodge's 27th Division on the 18th. Hodge summed it all up when he said: "It is going to be really tough. There are 65,000 to 70,000 fighting Japs holed up in the south end of the island, and I see no way to get them out except blast them out yard by does not know when he is bypassed."

Despite their failure in the attack of April 19 the Americans had no choice but to keep up the pressure on the Shuri defences. When the fighting died down with the coming of darkness on the 19th a gap of nearly a mile yawned between 27th and 96th Divisions and General Griner, commander of the 27th, knew that it must be plugged. But the attack of April 20 went the same way as that of the

19th. This time the problem was a Japanese strongpoint which squarely blocked the line of advance west of Gusukuma towards the Machinato airfield—a strongpoint which had got the very best out of the terrain, was heavily manned, and which had to be cleared out, not bypassed. The Americans called it "Item Pocket" and it took them another exhausting week before it fell. Impromptu names for the key landmarks—"Charlie Ridge", "Brewer's Hill", "Dead Horse Gulch"—became feared and hated names during the incessant fighting between April 20 and April 27, when the Pocket was eventually declared secure. Weeks later, however, Japanese were still emerging from the deep bolt-holes and caves which had given the position its strength.

In the meantime the 7th, 27th, and 96th Divisions battered away at the outer Shuri defences on the centre and left of the front. On the latter sector the Japanese had based their defence on "Skyline Ridge", blocking the approach to Unaha and Yonabaru airfield. In the centre, Kakazu Ridge was still in Japanese hands. While the fight for Item Pocket raged on the right flank, the Americans struggled painfully forward until at last, by April 24, they had taken both Kakazu and Skyline Ridges. After three weeks' ordeal the outer shell of the Shuri defences had finally been cracked.

At the end of April, Buckner reshuffled his front-line divisions, many units of which were badly in need of a rest. The 27th Division was relieved by the 1st Marine Division on April 30, and the 6th Marine also earmarked for a shift south to the front. The fall of Item Pocket on April 27 was followed by an exact replica of the preceding seven days—and then, on May 4, the Japanese unleashed a counter-offensive aimed at smashing the centre of 10th Army and driving its fragments into the sea. It was an ambitious plan, envisaging amphibious landings deep in the rear of the American positions—but it suffered the same fate as the earlier Japanese attack. The amphibious operation was a total fiasco. Despite a temporary breakthrough in the centre and the recapture of Tanabaru Ridge, the Japanese 24th Division had shot its bolt by the 7th and Ushijima had no choice but to fall back on the defensive, having achieved little but to delay the American advance for just under a week. (During the fighting for the Tanabaru Ridge the

◁◁ *After hurling an explosive into the mouth of a cave, a Marine patrol waits for any surviving Japanese to emerge.*
◁▽ *Fighting in the streets of Naha, Okinawa's main city. Many buildings were set on fire by Americans as the only way to flush out Japanese troops.*

△ *V.E. Day on Okinawa— while Europe celebrated, there was no respite for these Marines as the bitter struggle continued. One unit goes in as another pulls back from the fighting in Naha.*

news of the German surrender reached Okinawa. "Well, now," said a colonel of the 17th Infantry Division, as he sniped at the Japanese with an M1 carbine, "if we just had the Japs off the escarpment we'd be all right, wouldn't we?")

Once Ushijima's counter-atack had been safely held, Buckner saw in it a chance for a breakthrough. The attack had drawn the last fresh Japanese reserves into the line, and a prompt resumption of the initiative could well prove decisive. The result was the renewal of the attack on May 10 and its culmination on the 21st with the clearing of a "funnel" on the left flank which enabled the 7th Division to edge forwards into the inner ring of the Shuri defences. In this phase the decisive actions were the clearing of the eastern sides of Conical and Sugar Hills, which bent back the extreme right wing of the Japanese line. Plotted on a map, it seemed that the way was open for the rolling-up of the front from the east – but the Japanese remained in firm control of their positions and no breakthrough came. And now, in the fourth week of May, the elements sided with the Japanese. The rain poured down and the battle-field of Okinawa dissolved in mud.

Transport was paralysed and it was impossible to move heavy equipment through the floods and quagmires – but there was no diminution of the pressure. With the Japanese centre north of Shuri still rock steady, Buckner ordered the flanking divisions to intensify operations and bend back the Japanese wings as far as possible. It was an exhausting and undramatic process. With every day's new advances the "bulge" being formed round Shuri seemed to herald the total envelopment of Ushijima's men – but still the Japanese refused to break and the casualties continued to soar. With the rain and the mud and the pattern of attrition in men's lives (one dead American for every ten dead Japanese by the end of May) the battle of Okinawa was taking on the nature of the most hideous trench-warfare pounding match of World War I – and with as few obvious results.

Yet now at last the persistence of the Americans was rewarded. Even before the ominous constriction of the flanks of the 32nd Army in the last weeks of May, General Ushijima had made the decision to yield the Shuri Line and withdraw to the south after a conference with his staff on May 21. The consensus of opinion had been that to hold on at Shuri would only mean that the 32nd Army would be destroyed earlier than necessary, without having inflicted sufficient losses on the Americans. The 32nd Army would make its last stand at the southern tip of Okinawa. Supplies and wounded began moving south on the night of May 22-23, heading for the positions previously constructed by the 24th Division.

The Japanese retreat

With the rearguard holding on in front of Shuri, the Japanese pulled out with skill and discipline, and their move was largely completed by the end of May. The Japanese move was helped by the sluicing rains and the lowering overcast, which seriously impeded American aerial reconnaissance. From May 26, however, the long Japanese columns were kept under general surveillance from the air: and a 10th Army staff meeting on the evening of May 30 reached the conclusion that although the Japanese were still holding before Shuri, their line was little but a tough shell. It was widely believed that Ushijima had made his decision too late and that the campaign was all over bar the mopping-up. Once again it was a serious under-estimation of the actual situation. Shuri fell at long last on May 31, but Buckner's divisions did not, as expected, trap the 32nd Army in a pocket and wipe it out. Nor were they able to prevent it from pulling back and forming yet another solid front in the south. For this the Americans could certainly blame the adverse weather conditions: "We had awfully tough luck to get the bad weather at the identical time that things broke," lamented Buckner.

Thus the scene was set for the last round of the battle for Okinawa. The southern end of the island is best described as a downward-pointing arrowhead. The Shuri Line had crossed the shank of the arrowhead above the barbs; and now the 32nd Army had pulled right down into the very tip of the arrow. An amphibious operation coped with the western barb of the arrowhead, the Orotu Peninsula, trapping the remnants of Rear-Admiral Minoru Ota's naval troops and wiping them out by June 15 after a ten-day battle. Meanwhile the first attacks on the main Japanese position behind the Yaeju-Dake Ridge had begun.

It took five murderous days – June 12-

△ △ *Lieutenant-General Simon Bolivar Buckner* (left) *with Major-General Roy S. Geiger. A few days after this picture was taken, Buckner was killed by enemy fire and Geiger succeeded him as commander of the 10th Army.*
△ *On Okinawa an unusually large number of Japanese began to surrender. This officer decided to give himself up after hearing a broadcast from an offshore landing craft.*
▷ *Snatching a well-earned rest, two Marines sleep in a foxhole next to their machine gun.*

17–to crack the Yaeju-Dake position: five days in which the fighting was as intense as ever. The Japanese still had to be blasted and burned from their foxholes, and a new American flame-throwing tactic was to bring up a 200-foot fuel supply hose from which to spray napalm on Japanese positions. By June 17 the survivors of the 32nd Army had been blasted out of their front-line position and compressed into an area eight miles square. After more than two and a half months of superb endurance, the men of the 32nd Army had reached the end of their tether. Between the 18th and the 21st they were split into three independent pockets and it was obvious that the end was near. Buckner sent a personal appeal to Ushijima to see reason and save the lives of his last men. Ushijima received it with vast amusement. He radioed his last message to Tokyo on the evening of the 21st, and he and his chief-of-staff, General Isamu Ota, committed ritual *hara-kiri* the same night. The last organised resistance–on Hill 85, between Medeera and Makabe–was broken on the 21st. Although "Old Glory" was formally raised over Okinawa at the 10th Army headquarters on the morning of the 22nd, mopping-up operations lasted until the end of the month; and the Ryūkyūs campaign was officially declared ended on July 2.

The cost

The Allies had conquered Okinawa and were now only 350 miles from Kyūshū itself. The objective of "Iceberg" had been achieved, but at a terrifying cost. Total American battle casualties were 49,151. The Americans had lost 763 aircraft and 36 ships sunk; another 368 of their ships had been damaged. But the Japanese had lost 110,000 men, including conscripts and drafted civilians, and even this has to be an approximate figure. Only 7,400 Japanese prisoners were taken on Okinawa–most of them in the last days when the 32nd Army was disintegrating. Ten major *kamikaze* attacks had been thrown against Okinawa, using up some 1,465 aircraft; and the total number of suicide sorties was 1,900. The Japanese losses in aircraft were staggering: 7,800. The Imperial Navy lost 16 ships sunk and four damaged.

What did the Okinawa campaign prove?

▽ *Marines move cautiously over "Cemetery Ridge". Enemy snipers keep them pinned down, seeking cover among the gravestones.*

First and foremost, it gave a bitter foretaste of what the Allies could expect if they ever tried to land on Japanese soil. It was the bloodiest fight of the Pacific war. But above all it proved that nothing could stop the Allies in the Pacific from moving where they wanted, even if it did mean killing every Japanese in their way. And Ushijima himself paid tribute to this in his last message to Tokyo. "Our strategy, tactics, and technics all were used to the utmost and we fought valiantly," he reported. "But it was as nothing before the material strength of the enemy."

The end of Japan's Navy

After the Battle of Leyte Gulf in October 1944, the Japanese Combined Fleet could no longer be recognised as the proud and efficient fighting force which had gone to war in December 1941. It was a shrivelled husk, largely immobilised by lack of fuel. Never again after Leyte did the Combined Fleet concentrate its strength to fight the carrier task forces of the American and British Pacific fleets. But the surviving Japanese warships still had a part to play, and they remained high-priority targets for the Allies until the end of the war.

The Midway disaster of 1942 had caused the Japanese to adopt an accelerated and expanded carrier-building programme, but they never made good the losses of Coral Sea and Midway. The programme was a dual affair, including the construction of brand-new carriers from the keel up and the conversion of merchantmen and suitable warship hulls. Typical of the former category was the *Taiho*, lost in her first battle–the last big carrier clash of the Pacific war in the Philippine Sea (June 19, 1944) during the campaign in the Marianas. *Taiho* had actually been laid down before Pearl Harbor, but for months work on her had proceeded at a crawl. She displaced 29,300 tons, compared with the 25,675 tons of *Shokaku* and *Zuikaku*. She could achieve 33 knots and carried 74 aircraft (53 of them operational and 21 spare). But the details of her fate reveal the very great changes which had affected the Japanese carrier force between the days of Pearl Harbor and the last year of the war. The American submarine *Albacore* put a torpedo into *Taiho* on the morning of June 19. At first there seemed very little to worry about;

two fuel tanks had been ruptured and the flight-deck elevator jammed shut, but *Taiho* could still maintain full speed. The immediate hazard was the spreading fumes from the liberated oil and aviation spirit. The principal fuel of the vessel in 1944 was crude oil, as a result of overall shortages. The ship's ventilators were put on full blast in an attempt to dispel the fumes – a fatal decision. The fumes were spread throughout the vessel and continued to accumulate. The inevitable end came when a spark on the hangar deck detonated them. The effects were cataclysmic. A tremendous explosion shook *Taiho* from stem to stern, blowing

cannibalised from the uncompleted skeleton of "Hull III", the fourth "Yamato" class super-battleship (significant of the belated swing away from Japan's pre-war obsession with the big battleship as the prime mover of sea power). *Scharnhorst's* original electric turbines were retained; they were in fact only the second set to be used by a ship of the Imperial Navy. In her new guise, *Shinyo* finally joined the fleet in mid-December 1943. She was not present at the Battle of the Philippine Sea but was given a further eight 50-mm A.A. guns after that action, giving her a total of 50. Completely unarmoured, *Shinyo* had a best speed of 22 knots. Her air

out the hangar walls, ripping the flight deck, and perforating the ship's bottom. She sank within minutes, the victim of an elementary hazard of carrier life which had been obvious for years.

As for the second category of the "last generation" of Japanese carriers, a typical example may be cited with *Shinyo*. She started life as the German luxury liner *Scharnhorst*, which had been at Kobe since the outbreak of war in 1939. *Scharnhorst* was purchased by the Japanese Government in the months after Midway; she was renamed *Shinyo*, and her conversion was begun at the Kure Naval Yard in November 1942. Parts were

group consisted of a maximum of 33 planes: 27 operational and six spare. And she fell victim to the far-ranging American submarine arm, being torpedoed by the *Spadefish* in the China Sea on November 17, 1944.

Giant aircraft-carrier

But the biggest conversion job in the Japanese carrier programme was that of the giant *Shinano*, originally the third (after *Yamato* and *Musashi*) of the super-battleships. *Shinano's* whole story was

△ △ *Brigadier-General William J. Wallace* (left), *chief of fighter command, and Major-General Francis P. Mulcahy, commander of the 10th Army's Tactical Air Force, study the latest operations report at Yontan airfield, Okinawa.*
△ ◁ *Two men of the 1st Marines gaze down at a wounded*

Japanese soldier. At the bottom of the truck is a dead American.
△ *Just north of Naha, two U.S. Marines manhandle their bazooka into position.*
△▷ *With the plasma bottle hooked onto his rifle, a Navy Hospital Corpsman administers blood to a wounded Marine.*

one of monstrous error and wasted effort – much like the giant Japanese "I-400" submarines. To start with, argument raged for weeks over what sort of aircraft-carrier she should be: an orthodox carrier or a giant floating depot-ship and mobile base, carrying no aircraft of her own but able to supply and equip – and provide an additional flight-deck for – an entire carrier fleet. The final result was a compromise. *Shinano* would be a carrier supply-ship, but she would also have a few fighters of her own for self-defence and a hangar for storing them. This caused immense difficulties, because *Shinano's* hull had been completed up to the

by 131 feet. She could steam at 27 knots, she bristled with defensive armament, and she could carry 47 aircraft. At last, the backbone of Japan's new carrier fleet was finished – but the carrier fleet did not exist. There were carriers; there were aircraft; but there was little or no fuel for either, and certainly no trained aircrew. *Shinano* was, in fact, an awe-inspiring but thoroughly useless white elephant. And her end was little short of bathos. On November 28, 1944, she left Yokosuka for a brief shake-down cruise, escorted by three destroyers. She had not been at sea 24 hours, let alone moved out of sight of land, when she was caught by

main deck by the time of the decision to convert her. The work crawled along – as slowly, in fact, as did that on Germany's only aircraft-carrier, *Graf Zeppelin* – in a dreary stop-go rhythm. When the builders were finally galvanised into an all-out effort, after the defeat in the Philippine Sea, it was too late. All the reserves of trained aircrew had been whittled away to the point of extinction. Nevertheless, the work on the useless giant moved to completion and *Shinano* was ready for service in November 1944.

She was the biggest aircraft-carrier in the world, and the best protected. Her armoured flight-deck stretched 840 feet

the American submarine *Archerfish,* and hit by a salvo of four torpedoes.

In the Battle of Leyte Gulf, *Shinano's* sister-ship *Musashi* had proved what tremendous punishment the class could take and still stay afloat. *Musashi* had been singled out as the main target for American air attacks as Kurita's battle fleet struggled through the Sibuyan Sea. Plastered by bombs and ripped by repeated torpedo hits, she had refused to sink, and her expert crew kept her afloat by skilful counter-flooding for hours until the end. *Shinano* was not vitally damaged at all by *Archerfish's* torpedoes and could still make 18 knots. But her inexperienced

The Japanese battleship *Yamato*

Displacement: 64,200 tons.
Armament: nine 18.1-inch,
twelve 6.1-inch, twelve 5-inch A.A.,
146 25-mm A.A., and four 13-mm
guns, plus six aircraft.
Armour: 16-inch belt, 9-inch deck,
$25\frac{1}{2}$-inch turrets, and $19\frac{3}{4}$-inch
control tower.
Speed: 27 knots.
Radius: 7,200 miles at 16 knots.
Length: 863 feet.
Beam: $127\frac{3}{4}$ feet.
Draught: $34\frac{1}{4}$ feet.
Complement: 2,500.

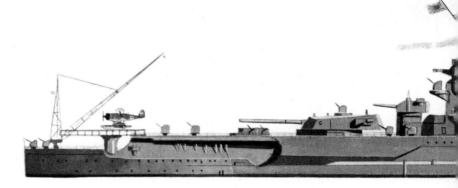

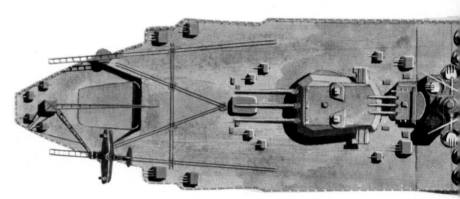

The Japanese aircraft-carrier *Shinano*

Displacement: 62,000 tons.
Armament: sixteen 5-inch and
145 25-mm A.A. guns, plus 336
5-inch rockets, and 47 aircraft.
Armour: $15\frac{3}{4}$-inch belt and
4-inch deck.
Speed: 27 knots.
Radius: 10,000 miles at 18 knots.
Length: $872\frac{3}{4}$ feet.
Beam: $131\frac{1}{4}$ feet.
Draught: $33\frac{3}{4}$ feet.
Complement: 2,400.

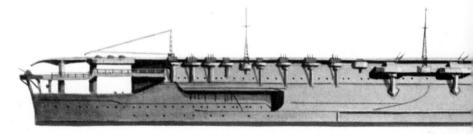

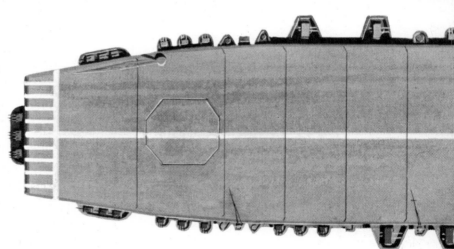

crew neglected practically every damage-control rule in the book. The waters rose and spread from compartment to compartment; she kept on her course at full speed; and her captain would certainly have been court-martialled for gross negligence if he had not gone down with *Shinano,* seven hours after the torpedoing, at 1017 on November 29.

Mobility and hitting-power are the prerequisites of a carrier force, and by 1945 the Japanese carrier force had no fuel and no aircrew. This in turn meant that the surviving units of the Imperial Navy were now finally denuded of their air umbrella and were, from a strategic point of view, little more than floating scrap-iron. The Americans went ahead with the last major offensives of the Pacific war—Luzon, Iwo Jima, and Okinawa—secure in the knowledge that the Japanese Navy would never pose a serious threat to them again.

To the Japanese high command it was unthinkable that the Emperor's last warships should be bombed to destruction in their home ports, or hunted down independently at sea. The *kamikaze* strategy was therefore applied to the Japanese Navy—but, as with the Army and Navy air forces, the problem remained one of *matériel*, not men. There were thousands of eager volunteers willing to show their veneration for their Emperor by immolating themselves on an enemy carrier and taking as many Americans with them as possible. The difficulty was in getting them there. The Navy, as we have seen, developed two main *kamikaze* weapons of its own: *kaiten* and explosive speedboats. However, the best suicide weapon remained the aircraft, plummeting down on its target from the skies.

Kamikaze mentality

The ambitious "*SHO*" plan which had thrown the massed strength of the Combined Fleet against the Americans at Leyte had been motivated by the *kamikaze* mentality: to do as much damage as possible with inferior resources. And the same held true of one of the most bizarre episodes in naval history: the suicide sortie of the *Yamato* during the opening phase of the long battle for Okinawa, in April 1945.

Japan's defensive strategy was based on the idea of "Dunkirking" the spearhead troops, once they had got ashore, and disrupting the Allied offensive plan by raising as much havoc as possible. And it was to this end that the "Special Sea Attack Force" was formed. It consisted of the *Yamato* and a light destroyer escort. Using literally the last dregs of the country's fuel oil stocks, the *Yamato* would make straight for the invasion beaches at Okinawa, deal out maximum destruction to the American invasion fleet, then beach herself and fight to the last shell available for her huge 18-inch guns.

Under the command of Vice-Admiral Seiichi Ito, the force sailed from Tokuyama in Japan's Inland Sea on the afternoon of April 6: *Yamato,* surrounded by a ring of eight destroyers and the light cruiser *Yahagi.* The Japanese squadron had barely cleared Japanese territorial waters before it was spotted by American submarines patrolling the Bungo Strait, between the islands of Shikoku and Kyūshū. Once out at sea, Ito altered course to the west, steering into the East China Sea preparatory to a last turn to the south for the final run down to Okinawa, and his ships were sighted at 0822 hours on the 7th by reconnaissance aircraft from Admiral Marc Mitscher's Task Force 58. A mighty strike of 380 dive-bombers and torpedo-bombers took off from Mitscher's carriers at 1000, when the Japanese force was some 250 miles away—just before *Yamato* and her frail ring of escorts swung to the south. Around noon the first contact was made and the final ordeal of the *Yamato* began.

The American pilots were impressed by the massive A.A. fire which came up at them: the Japanese had learned the lesson of air power well, and by the time of her last voyage *Yamato* bristled with no less than 146 25-mm A.A. guns. Most impressive of all, however, were the *San-Shiki* shells fired by her main armament, which may be best described as 18-inch shotgun shells. *Yamato's* main battery was designed for use in the anti-aircraft rôle and the *San-Shiki* shells were crammed with incendiary bullets. The idea was that the shells would be fired into a group of enemy aircraft; the shells would then burst, like a shotgun fired into a flock of birds, mowing down the enemy planes. It was found, however, that the terrifying blast of *Yamato's* 18-inch guns when fired at maximum elevation only served to disrupt the main volume of A.A. fire. The *San-Shiki* shells

proved to be a failure, like so many other impressive-sounding Japanese ideas.

The Japanese had the weather—squalls and low clouds—on their side, but little else. The Special Attack Force had no fighter cover whatever and the American bombers were able to make almost unimpeded practice as repeated waves swept in to the attack. The ring of Japanese destroyers soon broke up under the stress of constant manoeuvre to avoid torpedoes. Pounded to a wreck, *Yahagi* sank shortly after 1400 hours; and 25 minutes later came the turn of *Yamato*. She had taken a fearful beating; at least ten torpedoes had hit her, plus seven bombs. Her crew was unable to cope with the inrush of water, or keep her upright by counter-flooding. *Yamato* finally capsized and sank at 1425. Admiral Ito and nearly all the ship's company of 2,400 men went down with her. Four of the escorting destroyers were sunk as well, and the battered survivors turned for home.

An era ends

Such was the Battle of the East China Sea on April 7, 1945. It was the end of the Dreadnought age—the last time that a battleship was sunk by enemy action on the high seas. The wheel had indeed come full circle since Pearl Harbor in December 1941, when the superb Japanese carrier arm had proved the vulnerability of the battleship once and for all. *Yamato's* sacrifice was totally useless; she had never even sighted Okinawa, let alone taken any pressure off the gallant Japanese garrison there. On the Japanese side of the ledger there was only one completely insignificant flicker of success: a *kamikaze* hit on the American carrier *Hancock*.

Cowering in the Japanese home ports lay the remnants of the Imperial Navy. At Yokosuka there was the battleship *Nagato,* in her heyday the strongest battleship in the world with her 16-inch main armament. Her last action had been Leyte Gulf, where she had escaped the holocaust of the battleships. Now in the summer of 1945 she was inoperative, inglorious, with her funnel and foremast removed to assist camouflage. The rump of the battle fleet lay at Kure, Japan's great naval base. There were the *Ise* and *Hyuga,* absurdly converted to seaplane-carriers by the removal of their after

Okinawa

0   5   10 MILES

turrets. With equal absurdity they had been classified the 4th Carrier Division of the 2nd Fleet in November 1944. In March 1945 they had finally been taken off the active list and now served as A.A. batteries. Also at Kure was the *Haruna,* the last survivor of the "*Kongo*" class battle-cruisers built on the eve of World War I. With the *Kongos* Japanese designers had shown the world that they had seen through the inherent weaknesses of the battle-cruiser concept by specifying their order for fast battleships; and the *Kongos* had been extensively reconstructed between the wars. Another genuine museum-piece at Kure in 1945 was the old target-ship *Settsu,* whose construction had helped place Japan fourth after Britain, the United States, and Germany as a Dreadnought naval power.

Seven Japanese aircraft-carriers were also in home waters. First among them was the little *Hosho,* the first carrier in the world to be designed as such from the

△ *The American conquest of the Japanese island of Okinawa.*
△▷ *The mighty Japanese battleship* Yamato *during her fitting out in 1941.*

keel up, which had been launched after World War I. When she served as fleet carrier training ship, most of the Japanese Navy's crack aircrews learned their trade aboard her. She had survived Midway as Yamamoto's last serviceable carrier and was still in service in 1945. The other six carriers–*Ibuki, Amagi, Katsuragi, Kaiyo, Ryuho,* and *Junyo*–represented the losing struggle to restore carrier protection and hitting-power to the Combined Fleet. Apart from destroyers and submarines still in service, the only other major units of the Combined Fleet in Japanese ports in 1945 were six cruisers.

With American carrier planes now able to range at will over the Japanese homeland, it was only a matter of time before these sorry survivors were singled out for destruction. Admiral Halsey planned it personally: it was to be a formal revenge for Pearl Harbor, an all-American operation without the British Pacific Fleet. It took the form of a fearsome three-day blitz on the Japanese naval bases, concentrating on Kure. Between July 24 and 26, 1945, the American carrier forces struck round the clock. In those hectic days they sank the *Amagi, Ise* and *Hyuga, Haruna, Settsu,* and five cruisers, effectively destroying Japanese hopes of forming a possible suicide squadron from their last heavy warships. If any one date is required for the formal annihilation of the Japanese fleet, it may be set as July 24-26, 1945.

Midget craft

Although the British did not participate in the mass attacks on the Japanese naval bases, they were nevertheless active during this final phase. Ranging over the Inland Sea, British carrier planes sank two frigates and several other small fry, and also claimed a hit on an escort

The Japanese destroyer *Yukikaze*

Displacement: 2,033 tons.
Armament: six 5-inch and four
25-mm A.A. guns, plus eight
24-inch torpedo tubes.
Speed: 35 knots.
Radius: 5,000 miles at 18 knots.
Length: 388½ feet.
Beam: 35½ feet.
Draught: 12⅓ feet.
Complement: 240.

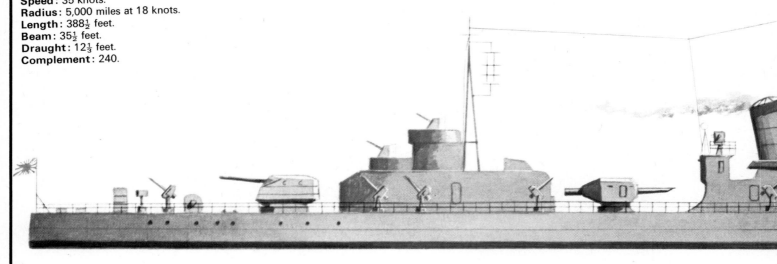

carrier. The biggest feather in the caps of the British, however, was earned thousands of miles away: in a dramatic and successful midget submarine attack on the port of Singapore.

At Singapore lay the Japanese heavy cruisers *Takao* and *Myoko*, both of them marked down for attack by the Sub-marine Flotilla of the British Pacific Fleet. Two XE-craft (improved versions of the midget submarine which had crippled the German battleship *Tirpitz* in her Arctic lair in late 1943 – were detailed for the job: *XE-1* (Lieutenant J. E. Smart) and *XE-3* (Lieutenant Ian Fraser). On July 30, 1945, the two midgets

were on their way to the approaches to Singapore Roads, towed by their parent submarines: *Spark* (*XE-1*) and *Stygian* (*XE-3*).

In the history of submarine warfare this attack is particularly interesting because of the use of the echo depth-finder in navigating to the target. By 0600 hours on July 31–set as the day for the attack–*XE-3* was manoeuvring up the Johore Strait at 30 feet. The boom–hardly a formidable affair, with a permanent gate some 300 yards wide–was safely passed at 1030 and the target, *Takao*, was sighted at 1250. As *XE-3* closed in on her victim there was a disconcerting moment. As Fraser put it, "I was very upset to see a motor cutter filled with Japanese liberty men only about 30 yards from my periscope." *XE-3*, however, remained undetected as she crawled towards *Takao* across the uneven harbour bottom, fetching up against the hull of the Japanese cruiser

with a loud clang at 1442 hours.

With great daring, Fraser decided to make his attack with *XE-3* wedged squarely beneath *Takao's* hull. The attack used two weapons: limpet mines, attached to the enemy hull by the XE-craft's diver, and fused explosive charges, released from the midget's hull from inside. Opera-

◁▽ Yamato *undergoing sea trials off Sata Point, October 30, 1941.*
▽ *Under attack from bomb- and torpedo-carrying planes of the U.S. Pacific Fleet,* Yamato *is surrounded by water fountains from near-misses. She finally sank in the East China Sea on April 7, 1945.*

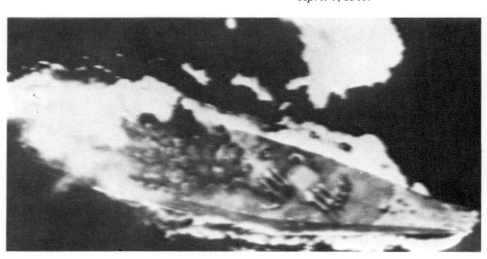

ting with great difficulty in the murky waters of the harbour, diver Leading-Seaman J. Magennis attached six limpets to *Takao's* bottom. It was a long and exhausting job, for he had to scrape off patches of weed and barnacles to get the limpets to stick. After placing the mines and returning inside *XE-3,* Magennis had to go back outside and release the starboard explosive charge, which refused to detach itself. Tired though he was, Magennis had no hesitation in immediately volunteering for this strenuous and extremely dangerous job. As Fraser's report has it: "He went on oxygen again at 16.25 hrs. and made his exit to the casing with a large spanner in his hand. After seven minutes he managed, by much banging at the carrier and levering at the release pins, to get the carrier away."

With the explosives safely placed in position, Fraser turned to the task of wriggling *XE-3* clear of her victim and retreating to the open sea for the rendezvous with *Stygian.* Despite several harrowing moments the retreat passed off safely. The boom was passed at 1949 hours and at 2100 *XE-3* was able to surface and proceed down the Johore Strait. Rendezvous was safely made with *Stygian* at 2345 hours.

Smart, in *XE-1,* had had bad luck from the start of the approach. One mishap after another had combined to delay his attack so badly that he risked being caught inside the boom if he had pressed on to his own target. Smart therefore took the extremely brave decision to attack Fraser's target as well and take the risk of being blown up by the detonation of *XE-3's* limpets and charges. The possibility of this was heightened by the fact that the detachable charges were fitted with disturbance fuses, and *XE-1* would stand a likely chance of setting them off. But the calculated risk taken by Smart paid off; he dropped his charges and retreated safely. A final mishap was a 24-hour delay in the rendezvous with *Spark.* Fraser and Magennis received the Victoria Cross for their attack, Smart the Distinguished Service Order.

As for the unfortunate *Takao,* left with two sets of explosive charges and six limpet mines, the resultant explosion effectively destroyed her as a fighting ship by blowing the bottom out of her.

◁ △ *Dropping supplies and . . .*
◁ *. . . picking them up in the beach-head area.*

The American Curtiss SB2C-3 Helldiver dive-bomber

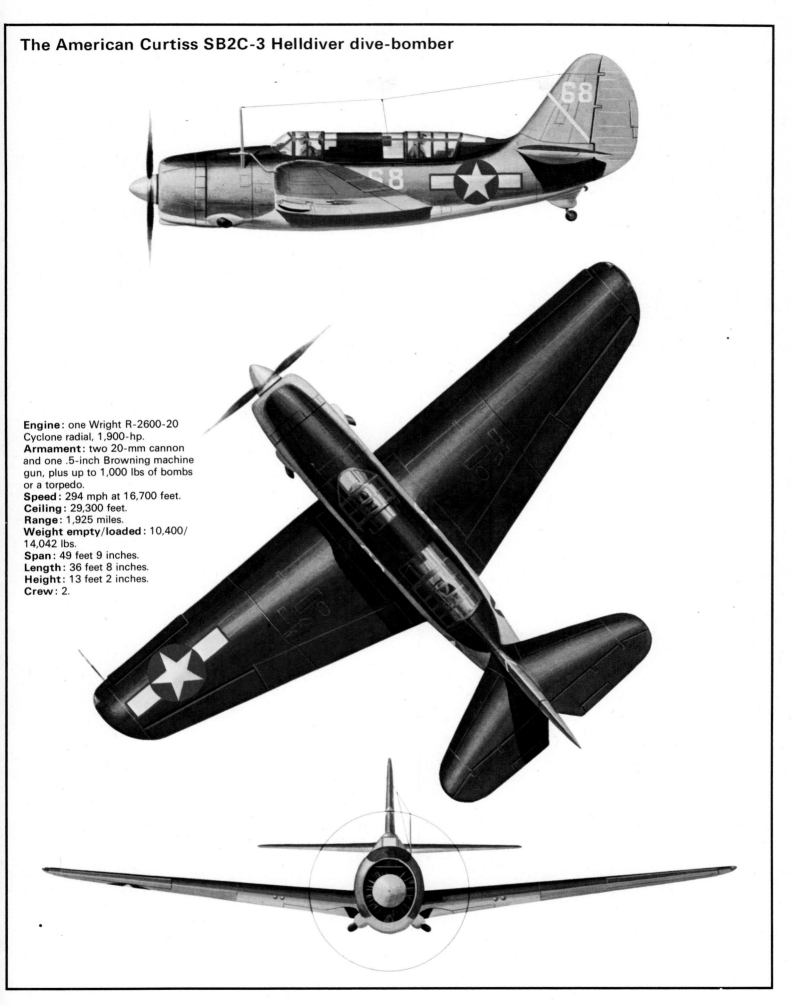

Engine: one Wright R-2600-20
Cyclone radial, 1,900-hp.
Armament: two 20-mm cannon
and one .5-inch Browning machine
gun, plus up to 1,000 lbs of bombs
or a torpedo.
Speed: 294 mph at 16,700 feet.
Ceiling: 29,300 feet.
Range: 1,925 miles.
Weight empty/loaded: 10,400/
14,042 lbs.
Span: 49 feet 9 inches.
Length: 36 feet 8 inches.
Height: 13 feet 2 inches.
Crew: 2.

Inglorious end

The postwar fate of the Japanese warships which survived Halsey's Blitz of
July 1945 was inglorious. *Nagato,* last of
the battle fleet, was used as a target ship
during the Bikini Atoll atom test in 1946,
together with the cruiser *Sakawa.* The
other cruisers and carriers were either
used as targets, scrapped, or sunk at sea
by the victors–the Americans in particular sank a hecatomb of surrendered
Japanese submarines off Gato Island in
April 1946.

The fate of the last vessels of the
Imperial Japanese Navy was the grim
end to a remarkable story. Japan's emer-
gence as a modern power only dates from
the last three decades of the 19th Century.
By careful study of the best European
models, she built a navy second to none
in either *matériel* or fighting spirit in
under 30 years. In that period Japanese
naval designers not only participated in
the birth of the Dreadnought era: they
proved again and again that they could
lead the world in laying down new concepts for the development of the fighting
ship and the evolution of naval warfare.

What went wrong? It is now generally
accepted that Japan's decision to go to
war in December 1941 was a calculated
risk, a gamble which came within an ace
of success. But as far as the total defeat
of her prime instrument of war in the
Pacific–the Combined Fleet–is concerned, several serious errors stand out.
The first is that in 1941 the Combined
Fleet was a contradiction in terms. Its

◁ ◁ A Sherman tank flame-
thrower of the 32nd Regiment,
7th Division, in action against a
cave atop Hill 95.
◁ During the rainy season: a
Marine Hospital ambulance jeep,
stuck fast in the semi-liquid mud,
is hauled out by a caterpillar
tractor. In the background a
tank destroyer stands by.
▷ Men of the 6th Marine
Division take a much-needed
opportunity to wash their clothes
– and themselves – in a bomb
crater on Naha airfield. Note the
wrecked Japanese aircraft in the
background.
▽ Marines move cautiously in
after throwing a smoke grenade
into a cave suspected of holding
Japanese troops.

carrier force was superb but the battle
fleet – the big gun – was still looked to as
the weapon which would bring decisive
victory. Submarine strategy was totally
misguided on the Japanese side, whereas
the Americans used their submarines
correctly and reaped the rewards. Above
all, however, the Japanese naval strate-
gists had to cut their coat according to
their cloth: the one thing they could not
afford was a war of attrition, and this
they got. The Guadalcanal campaign,
for example, cost them the equivalent of
an entire peace-time fleet – losses which
could never be replaced. The very speed
with which the Americans assumed the
offensive in the Pacific, never to lose it,
showed what a narrow margin the Japanese Navy had.

And the result was an unreal metamor-
phosis which led the Japanese into building huge white elephants like *Shinano*
and the aircraft-carrying "I-4400" submarines. It saw the Combined Fleet change
from an instrument of the offensive and
of victory to a sacrificial victim whose
purpose was only to stave off defeat.
This process first became dominant at
the time of the Marianas campaign in
June 1944, and it was the *leitmotif* of the
final destruction of the Combined Fleet.
That there was great heroism among the
men who took *Yamato* out on her last
voyage cannot be doubted. But the former
cold professionalism which had carried
the Japanese Navy to its high tide of
victory in the summer of 1942 was gone.
In ships, in men, and in men's ideas, too
much had been lost in the disastrous
naval operations in the Solomon Islands,
at Midway, and in the battle of Leyte Gulf.

▷ *The debris of war: Okinawan women and children rounded up by a party of Marines after the fighting.*
▽ *Deciding after all that dishonour is better than death, a group of Japanese soldiers surrenders to a U.S. Marine. Note the extreme youth of the soldier at far right.*

CHAPTER 171

BURMA: the Arakan Campaigns

In the jungle-covered belt of hills separating Burma from India the 1942 monsoon had effectively separated the British–Indian forces from the Japanese and given the former some respite after their long retreat.

However, General Wavell, the Commander-in-Chief in India, wanted to regain the initiative as soon as possible. On September 17, 1942 he issued an operation instruction to the G.O.C.-in-C. Eastern Army, Lieutenant-General N. M. S. Irwin, which gave the objects for the army in the 1942–1943 dry season (October–May): first to develop communications for the purpose of reconquering Burma and opening the Burma Road; and second to bring the Japanese to battle in order to use up their strength, especially in the air.

Wavell gave four objectives as his immediate intention in order to attain these ends:

1. to capture Akyab and reoccupy tl upper Arakan;
2. to strengthen British positions in tl Chin hills;
3. to occupy Kalewa and Sittaung on tl Chindwin; and thence to raid Japanes lines of communication (Wavell ha already given Brigadier Orde Winga orders to raise and train a Long Rang Penetration Brigade for this purpose and
4. to make necessary administrative a rangements to allow for a rapid advan into upper or lower Burma shoul opportunity offer.

We are here immediately concerne with the first objective, the British attem to capture Akyab in the dry season 1942 43. Throughout this narrative it is in portant to remember that the Japanes forces in the Arakan were seasoned vi torious soldiers, operating under battl tested commanders, forming homoge eous units which had fought in China an taken a major part in the successful co quest of Burma, whereas the British an Indian units had not previously been i action, had many new recruits and ha originally been trained and equipped fo a different type of warfare.

The Japanese 213th Regiment in th Arakan, under the command of Colon K. Miyawaki and consisting of two ba talions (II/213th and III/213th), had move into Akyab during the summer of 194 after chasing the British/Indian force from Yenangyaung, Myingan, Monywa Shwegyin, and finally Kalewa, which i had captured on May 11. The 33r Division, of which it formed a part, ha advanced from Siam for the initial ir vasion of Burma, but the 213th Regimen had been left in Siam and had not r joined its division until after the fall c Rangoon. It was, therefore, the freshes regiment and had had the fewest casua ties in the conquest of Burma and wa full of fight.

As the British/Indian 14th Divisio started its southward advance from Chi tagong to Cox's Bazar and beyond, Miya waki in mid-October sent his II/213t battalion up the Mayu river by launch t occupy the line Buthidaung–"Tunnels Road–Maungdaw, where first contac was made with the 1/15th Punjab bat talion on October 23. The "Tunnels Road was the only all-weather road in th area in 1942.

On September 21 Lieutenant-Genera Irwin had ordered the 14th Indian Div

Previous page: *Having pushed down the slopes of the Mayu Ridge, south of the Maungdaw-Buthidaung road on the Arakan front, men of a British battalion consolidate their position.*
▽ *Men of the Tripura Rifles cross a stream in the Arakan. This regiment had just completed six months of guerrilla warfare in the Kaladan valley.*

◁ *This photograph amply
illustrates the difficult terrain
that troops had to cope with
throughout the Burma campaign.*
△ *Lieutenant-General Shojiro
Iida, the Japanese commander in
Burma.*

▽ *Colonel Tai Koba led the
"Koba" Force, part of "Sakurai"
Column.*

△ *Lieutenant-General Tadashi Hanaya.*

▽ *The disastrous first campaign in the Arakan.*

sion, commanded by Major-General W. L. Lloyd, to move towards Akyab to forestall the Japanese arrival on the Buthidaung–Maungdaw line.

Earlier in the year the 14th Division had been earmarked for operations in Burma, but the fall of Rangoon had prevented its arrival. After the British defeat in Burma a special committee had reported that one of the reasons for this defeat was the over-modernisation of Indian divisions. Certain divisions were, therefore, reorganised to become "light divisions" with their transport mainly on a jeep and animal basis. The 14th Division, which had recently been responsible for the defence of Bengal, Bihar, and Orissa, was not so reorganised.

This division consisted of four brigades (47th, 55th, 88th, and 123rd), with two British and ten Indian battalions plus one British field regiment and one Indian mountain regiment of artillery. The Indian battalions came mainly from the dry

areas of the Punjab, Baluchistan, and Rajputana and were unused to the hot, steamy, malarial swamps of the Arakan. Later another brigade joined the division. For this rôle the 14th Division was supported by a special reconnaissance force ("V" Force) hidden, with its wireless sets, in the hills, and No. 2000 Flotilla, a scratch collection of steamboats, launches, and sampans, to help the units across and down the rivers and to supply them.

The Arakan, on Burma's north-west coast, is a country of steep, densely forested hill ranges up to 2,000 feet high running parallel from north to south separated by narrow cultivated valleys filled with rice fields, mangroves, and tidal creeks. The coastal strip from Maungdaw to the tip of the Mayu peninsula, Foul Point, opposite Akyab Island, is 45 miles long and ten miles wide in the north but tapers down to a few hundred yards wide at Foul Point.

To the east winds the Mayu river (called the Kalapanzin in its upper reaches) flanked by swamps of elephant grass and bamboo, and divided by knife-edged limestone ridges, 150 feet high.

East of the Mayu valley rises the great jumbled mass of the Arakan Tracts reaching as far as the Kaladan river valley, and 2,500 feet high. Further east again are the Arakan Yomas.

In the dry season, fair-weather tracks for wheeled vehicles can be made over the dry paddy fields and along the coastal strip at low tide. From mid-May to October the annual 200-inch rainfall is almost unceasing, with malaria and other tropical diseases hyperendemic. In the dry season from November to March the weather is delightful.

As it advanced, the 14th Division's line of communication from railhead was by sea from Chittagong to Cox's Bazar, motor transport to Tumbru, sampans on the Naf river to Bawli Bazar, and pack transport onwards.

In spite of reinforcements of motor launches, landing craft, and three paddle-steamers given to him, Major-General Lloyd by November 17 could still guarantee the maintenance of only four battalions to attack the Japanese. Being able to apply superior strength was always a problem for the British in the Arakan.

The Japanese, although outnumbered, were much better trained in watermanship and were thus able to take full

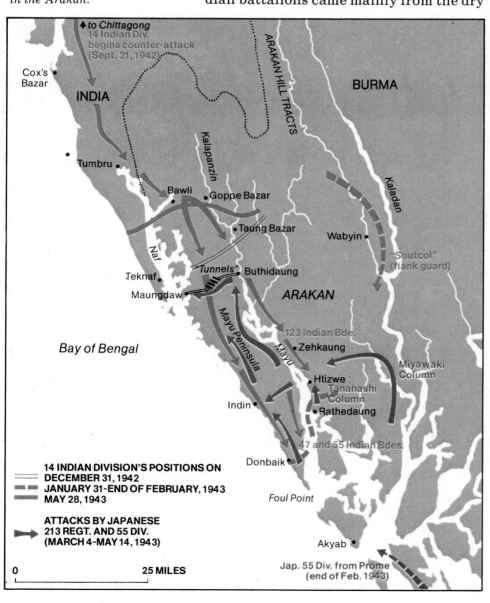

to Chittagong
14 Indian Div. begins counter-attack (Sept. 21, 1942)

Cox's Bazar

INDIA

Tumbru

Bawli

Kalapanzin

Goppe Bazar

Taung Bazar

ARAKAN HILL TRACTS

BURMA

Kaladan

Wabyin

"Soutcol" (flank guard)

Naf

Teknaf

"Tunnels" Buthidaung

Maungdaw

ARAKAN

Bay of Bengal

Mayu Peninsula

Mayu

123 Indian Bde.

Zehkaung

Miyawaki Column

Htizwe
Tanahashi Column

Indin

Rathedaung

47 and 55 Indian Bdes.

Donbaik

Foul Point

Akyab

Jap. 55 Div. from Prome (end of Feb. 1943)

14 INDIAN DIVISION'S POSITIONS ON
DECEMBER 31, 1942
JANUARY 31–END OF FEBRUARY, 1943
MAY 28, 1943

ATTACKS BY JAPANESE
213 REGT. AND 55 DIV.
(MARCH 4–MAY 14, 1943)

0   25 MILES

advantage of all types of river transport, especially as Akyab Island was at the hub of the river system running north. Thus their water communication could easily be switched from one valley to another, whereas the British lines of approach were divided by virtually inaccessible ridges.

In December 1942, the Japanese air situation in the south-west Pacific had become so grave that two Japanese air brigades were despatched from Burma, leaving the 5th Air Division with only about 50 fighters and 90 medium bombers available for the whole of the Burma front – to meet a growing Allied air strength.

No. 224 Group, R.A.F., consisting of six Hawker Hurricane squadrons, two light bomber squadrons of Bristol Blenheims and Bisleys, and one Beaufighter squadron (totalling about 120 aircraft), was ordered to support the 14th Division's advance. But at that time these squadrons had not been trained in close air support, the Hurricanes were not fitted with bomb racks, and there were no ground controllers with the brigades, so the group's efforts were initially of little value to the infantry (especially in comparison with

later operations). Thus the group's aircraft were used chiefly for interdiction along the sparse Japanese supply routes, including the sea-lanes to Akyab. In fact, during the first year the R.A.F. had very little effect on the ground campaign apart from moral support by the sound of the engines. Except at high altitude the Hurricane was no match for the Mitsubishi A6M Zero, and the R.A.F. had no long-range fighters available to sustain an offensive against the Japanese air bases. In spite of this the R.A.F. did slowly begin to win air superiority, which made efficient close air support, as well as vital air supply, possible later.

All these administrative and training shortcomings of the British forces must be remembered, as otherwise it is difficult to understand how Colonel Miyawaki, with a maximum of only two battalions on the mainland, could hold up 12 battalions of infantry supported by six batteries of artillery for a period of 13 weeks from first contact on October 23 to January 22 1943, when the first detachments of the 55th Division started to arrive in the Akyab area. The difficulty Lloyd had was to apply his strength.

Irwin's original plan was for a sea-

△ *During the tense days of February 1944, when the British front-line divisions were isolated from each other by the Japanese counter-attack: two men of the 1st Punjab Regiment – a Sepoy behind the Bren gun and Lance-Naik Ghulam Ali – lie up in a forward position overlooking the 7th Indian Division's "Admin. Box".*

borne landing on Akyab accompanied by a land advance down the Mayu peninsula to Foul Point. But by the end of October Wavell came to the conclusion that a direct seaborne attack in which transport and warships would be exposed to heavy air attack for a minimum of three days was no longer practicable.

Irwin therefore decided to use the 6th Infantry Brigade Group from the British 2nd Division to land on Akyab Island with the help of five motor launches, 72 landing craft, and three paddle-steamers which Admiral Sir James Somerville had placed at his disposal, as soon as Lloyd had advanced to Foul Point. The speed of the overland advance was therefore vital.

However, Irwin postponed Lloyd's advance to the attack in order to give him time to improve his communications, so that he could bring an extra brigade to bear. This delayed Lloyd by three weeks so that just when he was about to attack, Miyawaki withdrew his II/213th battalion facing Lloyd to a general line Gwedauk–Kondon, thus drawing Lloyd further away from his base.

Lloyd finally made contact again on December 22, when he attacked on either side of the Mayu range and also detached one battalion to the Kaladan river. The Japanese repulsed all attacks but the wide front forced Miyiwaki to commit his only other battalion, the III/213th, on December 29. Further British attacks were repulsed. The confident Japanese, having now got a measure of their enemy, started to harass Lloyd's two forward brigades by small patrol attacks at night and sudden bombardments from mortars, which startled these inexperienced troops and led them to believe that there were many more Japanese opposing them than just two battalions. Miyawaki, however, during this period took the risk of leaving the defence of Akyab Island to his anti-aircraft gunners, supported by administrative personnel.

During a visit with Wavell to the Donbaik front on December 10, Irwin criticised Lloyd for dispersing his force so widely that he had insufficient strength on the coast. He ordered Lloyd to concentrate and break through at Donbaik.

However, two more attacks by the 14th Division on their two objectives, Rathedaung and Donbaik, during the first two weeks in January, again failed. Repeated attacks by fresh troops on January 18 and 19 also failed with comparatively heavy losses.

But early in January, Lieutenant-General Shojiro Iida, commanding the 15th Army, realising the importance of and threat to, Akyab ordered Lieutenant-General Takishi Koga to move his 55th Division to hold Akyab. The 55th Division was a battle-trained formation which had fought in China and then advanced from Siam to Burma in 1942. During the previous year, it had fought through from Moulmein in the south via Pegu, Toungoo and Mandalay to Bhamo and the Chinese frontier.

Koga ordered a rapid overland advance via Pakokku to the Kaladan valley on the one hand, whilst at the same time opening up an administrative sea route from Toungup to Akyab. He ordered Miyawaki's 213th Regiment to hold the Rathedaung–Laungchaung–Donbaik line at all costs. On January 22 No. 224 Group R.A.F. attacked the Japanese columns on the Pakokku trail.

Irwin reinforced Lloyd with two fresh brigades, artillery, and eight Valentine tanks. On February 1, after a heavy but badly co-ordinated R.A.F. bombardment these fresh troops with the Valentines attacked the Japanese dug-in position at Donbaik, but after repeated assaults and heavy casualties over two days, were thrown back. Two days later similar frontal attacks on Rathedaung also failed.

The Japanese had won the race to Akyab, for by the end of February Koga

had assembled the whole of the 55th Division, less one battalion, in that area.

Iida expected Koga to consolidate, but the latter saw the six British/Indian brigades under Lloyd split up by rivers and ranges into three quite separate identities, with his own forces holding a central position at the confluence of the Arakan rivers. Koga realised that it was an excellent opportunity to counter-attack these tired brigades and destroy them piecemeal.

Koga laid a three-phase plan. First, the enemy forces in the Kaladan valley were to be overwhelmed by the "Miyawaki" Column (one infantry battalion and one mountain artillery battalion). Then the brigade east of the Mayu river was to be encircled by the "Tanahashi" Column (two infantry battalions and one mountain regiment) operating from Rathedaung and supported by a flank advance by Miyawaki from the Kaladan. Finally, the combined forces of this right hook, re-supplied by launches moving up the Mayu, would cross the river and the Mayu range to seize Indin. This would cut off the British/Indian brigades threatening the Donbaik–Laungchaung line. Koga left one battalion to hold Akyab and three battalions ("Uno" Column) to hold the Mayu peninsula.

Meanwhile, Lloyd was reorganising for another attack on Donbaik, but Irwin, aware of supply difficulties and danger from the east flank, ordered him to withdraw, intending to replace his division with the 26th. However, Wavell, egged on by Churchill, felt that it was essential for the morale of the whole Indian Army to score some sort of victory, rather than ignominiously retreat after suffering, by European standards, quite minor casualties. On February 26 Wavell directed Irwin to order Lloyd to attack Donbaik again with two brigades and to destroy "the numerically insignificant opposition". Irwin delayed the attack but also the withdrawal.

By February 21 the first phase of Koga's plan started.

By March 7 the "Miyawaki" Column had cleared the Kaladan valley as far as Kyauktaw, and "Tanahashi" Column had captured Rathedaung. The British/Indian 5th Brigade, with six battalions, obeyed Wavell's orders and carried out a deliberate attack on March 18 on the "Uno" Column dug in at Donbaik, but fell back after receiving only 300 casualties out of the 6,000-strong attacking force. With the

"Miyawaki" and "Tanahashi" Columns now poised on the east bank of the Mayu river, and the "Uno" Column as the anvil, having withstood the British attack at Donbaik, Koga launched the third phase of his attack, starting on the night March 24–25. He called for and was given all available air support from the 5th Air Division.

Tanahashi sent one battalion north-west, which cut the coastal road at Gyin-daw, whilst he, with the remaining two battalions of his force, advanced on Indin. In spite of a strenuous counter-attack and exhortations from their commanders, the brigades of the 14th Division on the coastal plain were unable to stop Tana-hashi, who occupied Indin on April 6, thus cutting off 11 British/Indian bat-talions and attached troops south of that point. After an attack by a third brigade from the north had failed to remove this block, the 6th Brigade managed to escape with its transport along the beach at low tide, but the 47th Brigade had to leave all its transport and guns and retreat in small dispersal groups through the jungle.

Lieutenant-General Koga had com-pleted his three-phase encirclement of th British/Indian brigades in one calenda month, exactly according to plan, and ha inflicted severe casualties on a muc larger force. With seven battalions an one pack regiment of artillery he ha temporarily destroyed the 47th Brigad and defeated the 4th, 6th, and 71st Brig ades with their three regiments of artiller (totalling seven British and ten India battalions).

With the arrival of his fresh II/214t battalion, which completed the strengt of his division, Koga, who saw his enem reeling, asked Iida if he could continu to attack until the monsoon. Iida, wh trusted Koga, gave him *carte blanche*.

Meanwhile, Lloyd had been replaced b Major-General C. E. N. Lomax and hi 26th Division headquarters. Lieutenan General Slim, commander of XV India Corps, whose duties during the past seve months had been to suppress the viciou insurgency campaign in Bengal led by th Indian Congress Party, which had state categorically that they would prefer Ja anese to British rule, was placed in overa command of the Arakan front on April

Slim had been in active command of the British/Indian forces in their 1,000-mile retreat from Burma the previous year and, as was his wont, had learnt much from his victorious, pugnacious enemy, who was trained to expect to fight against all odds. Slim found a most unsatisfactory state of affairs. Most of the units now under command of the 26th Division had had their morale lowered by abortive attacks on Rathedaung and Donbaik, and then had been eased out of their own defensive positions by the Japanese capacity for manoeuvres, flank attacks, and ability to bring all their weapons and troops, however inferior in numbers, to bear at a decisive point. All units, especially the Indian ones, were frustrated and bewildered and, as the British official history states, "the morale of the troops was generally poor and in some units very low".

Slim ordered Lomax to hold the Maungdaw-"Tunnels"-Buthidaung line. He reinforced Lomax's four brigades (4th, 6th, 55th, and 71st) with the 36th Brigade, bringing the force to a total of 19 battalions including seven British, 11 Indian, and one Gurkha.

Meanwhile, General Koga had eight battalions available for attack. He left one battalion to contain the British forces on the coastal strip, and one battalion with a mountain artillery regiment ("Miyawaki" Column) to hold his enemy east of the Mayu river. He divided his remaining six battalions, each supported by pack artillery, into "Uno" and "Tanahashi" Columns, and gave them the task of seizing Buthidaung and the Tunnels line and then wheeling left to capture Maungdaw. At this juncture the "Miyawaki" Column, east of the Mayu, would advance due north and capture Taung Bazar. The Japanese started their advance on April 23.

The "Uno" Column met with stubborn resistance at Kanthe, so the "Tanahashi"

△ ◁ *The effect of a smoke grenade thrown by Garhwali troops against a Japanese bunker in Maungdaw.*
◁ ◁ *Major-General H. C. Stockwell, commander of the 82nd West African Division, keeps his feet dry. With an offshore H.Q. on Stella, such trips to and from a waiting dinghy were frequent.*
△ *Brigadier Cotterill-Hill, 71st Indian Brigade, wades ashore during the invasion of Ramree Island.*
◁ *The second Arakan campaign.*

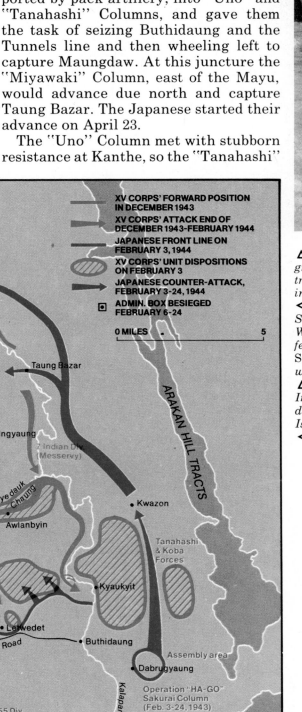

• Bawli Bazar
81 West African Div. (Woolner)
• Goppe Bazar
Goppe Pass
XV Corps (Christison)
MAYU RANGE
5 Indian Div. (Briggs)
Koba Force
• Myauke
Taung Bazar
Tanahashi Force
• Ingyaung
Laung Chaung
7 Indian Div. H.Q.
7 Indian Div. (Messervy)
Ngakyedauk Chaung
ARAKAN HILL TRACTS
• Kwazon
• Wabyin
Ngakyedauk Pass
Sinzweya
• Awlanbyin
5 Indian Div. H.Q.
Tanahashi & Koba Forces
• Kyaukyit
• Letwedet
Doi Column
"Tunnels" Road
• Buthidaung
Assembly area
• Dabrugyaung
Kalapanzin
Operation "HA-GO" Sakurai Column (Feb. 3-24, 1943)
Maungdaw
• Razabil
Jap. 55 Div. (Hanaya)

	XV CORPS' FORWARD POSITION IN DECEMBER 1943
	XV CORPS' ATTACK END OF DECEMBER 1943-FEBRUARY 1944
	JAPANESE FRONT LINE ON FEBRUARY 3, 1944
	XV CORPS' UNIT DISPOSITIONS ON FEBRUARY 3
	JAPANESE COUNTER-ATTACK, FEBRUARY 3-24, 1944
⊡	ADMIN. BOX BESIEGED FEBRUARY 6-24

0 MILES   5

Column by-passed Kanthe by advancing
along the razor beak Mayu range and
seized Point 551 overlooking the Tunnels
area of the Maungdaw–Buthidaung Road.
Lomax cleverly formed an open box to
trap the advancing Japanese between his
4th and 6th Brigades to the west, 55th
Brigade to the east, and 71st Brigade to
the north, forming the lid. The Japanese,
however, launched their northward drive
in earnest on May 2 and, by May 3, the
sides of the box had crumbled and the lid
had opened "without adequate reason".
The plan was a good one, but the training
and morale of the British/Indian troops
inevitably led to its failure.

As Buthidaung and the Tunnels area
fell to the Japanese, Slim, realising how
badly his superior forces had once again
been defeated in the jungle, wanted to
retreat 60 miles right back to Cox's
Bazar, into open country where he felt his
troops could oppose the Japanese on
ground more suitable to their training
and armament. However, Irwin stopped
this idea of wholesale withdrawal and
ordered Slim to hold the line Bawli Bazar
–Goppe Bazar–Taung Bazar, only 20 miles
north of the line Maungdaw–Buthidaung, and gave Lomax a sixth brigade,
with orders to prepare a counter-attack
to retake Maungdaw by surprise. But

Slim played for time until the arrival of
the monsoon stopped any further fighting.

By May 11 General Koga had again
won a striking victory over superior
forces. The partial failure of the British
demolition plan, and the disappearance in
panic of all the civilian labour on which
the British/Indian forces relied overmuch,
resulted in very large quantities of booty
falling into his hands. In view of the
depth of the British retreat and the
arrival of the monsoon, Koga decided to
take up a defensive position on the general
line Buthidaung–Maungdaw with five
battalions and a regiment of artillery and
withdraw the remainder of his division to
Akyab for rest and recuperation. In 16
weeks he had caused his enemy to suffer
over 5,000 battle casualties.

Severe criticism

The news of the British failure in the
Arakan, resulting in the loss of Buthidaung and Maungdaw, reached Washington just when the "Trident" Conference,
which had been called to decide on future
Allied policy in South-East Asia, was
taking place. General Wavell, the Indian
Army commander, and the commanders in
the Arakan all came under most severe
criticism. Churchill ordered that new
commanders must be found and battalions whose morale had broken should
be severely disciplined. If, he said, Indian
Army troops were incapable of fighting in
the jungle, commando formations should
be formed as a prototype and an example
to show them how to fight. Answers from
India were that the Indian Army had been
grossly over-expanded since Pearl Harbor
and the best Indian units were in the
Middle East, leaving a "second class
army" to oppose the Japanese. Jungle
fighting required, above all, good infantry
but the infantry had also been milked of
its best and most intelligent men to form
technical corps like the expanded Indian
artillery, previously manned wholly by
the British. Indian troops had had their
loyalty undermined by subversion from
the newly formed Indian Independence
League with its Indian National Army
fighting alongside the Japanese. British
officers drafted into the Indian Army had
not had time to learn the language and
get to know their men. Reinforcements to
replace battle and malarial casualties had
arrived piecemeal and many of them half-

rained. Some units had been left in the front line for many months without relief. Congress-sponsored riots in August and September 1942, accompanied by mal-istribution of food as a result of their depredations and destruction of communications, resulted in widespread famine in which 4 million had died, and this led to a disaffection amongst reinforcements moving through these areas to the battle line, so that they spread subversion amongst the forward troops.

Wavell was only too well aware that the failure in the Arakan, following as it did the disastrous campaigns in Malaya and Burma, had dealt the army in India a severe shock. Yet he knew that the Japanese were not "invincible" and had shown grave weaknesses of which advantage could be taken by a better trained army reinforced with self-confidence and self-respect. One undoubted advantage gained by the British was that during the year the R.A.F. had begun to attain air superiority throughout the whole front. This in itself could be made into a battle-winning factor. The success of the first Chindit operation, with its total reliance on air supply, offset the failures in the Arakan and pointed the way to victory in the future.

Wavell appointed a special committee to report on the readiness for war of British and Indian infantry battalions in India, and to make recommendation for improvement.

A new command set-up was created. Wavell was promoted Viceroy of India to look after the civil side and to see that the population would support its armed forces.

General Sir Claude Auchinleck was recalled from the Middle East to be C.-in-C. India and to make the Indian sub-continent into an efficient administrative and training base from which the fighting forces could draw their strength. He eventually created a self-confident new model Indian Army which became one of the best fighting machines in the world by 1945.

Lord Louis Mountbatten, who had previously been head of Combined Operations in Britain, was put in command of all the fighting forces in South-East Asia with his headquarters in Ceylon.

Brigades were to be formed of one British, one Indian, and one Gurkha battalion. Much more reliance was to be placed on the redoubtable Gurkhas, who had been represented by only one battalion in the Arakan débâcle.

After the first Chindit operation had proved the reliability of air supply, this form of support would be developed and

taught to all units so that they need never retreat or disintegrate if the Japanese go behind them.

The R.A.F. was persuaded to co-operate more fully in developing more reliable and accurate close air support for the army involving more intimate mutual signal arrangements and co-operation so that aircraft could take the place of artillery where necessary in the deep jungle.

All ranks were given more jungle, river, and night training so that they could feel that these features were on their side and not against them.

Rations and methods of cooking in the forward areas were improved so that detachments could fend for themselves for many weeks, and special rations were issued during training to build up men before operations so that they were capable of enduring long periods of duress.

Malaria, which was causing a hundred times more casualties than bullets or shells, was tackled by mepacrine, strict anti-malarial measures, and forward malarial treatment centres so that men needing treatment were not evacuated to base areas but remained in the line as a reserve to protect communications. This reform was one of the most effective means of ensuring that battalions in the line maintained their strength.

An illustration of the disproportionate losses from diseases is the British XXXIII Corps' casualty figures for June to November 1944, which were typical of all formations in this theatre:
Battle casualties 3,289
Sickness 47,098 (including 20,430 malaria cases).

These remedial actions have been emphasised because they were to turn the scales in the Arakan in 1944 when the Japanese for a third time launched their short range penetration forces with again it must be added, numerically very much inferior forces. Also it must be remembered that if the Japanese had had air superiority and as good air support, air supply, and intercommunication as the British were to enjoy the outcome might have been very different.

The results of the British command reorganisation was that General Sir George Giffard was appointed commander of an 11th Army Group, with Lieutenant-General William Slim, commander of the 14th Army, as one of his subordinates. XV Corps, under Lieutenant-General A. F. P. Christison, operating in the Arakan, came under Slim's command.

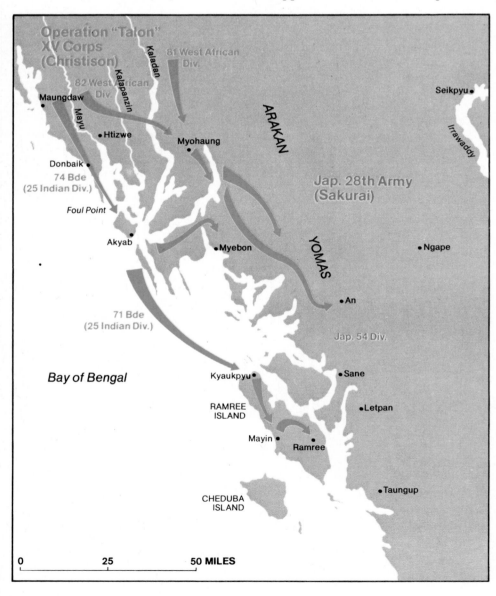
▽ *The third Arakan campaign.*

XV Corps in November 1943 consisted of the 5th and 7th Indian Divisions with 81st West African Division (less one brigade) in the Kaladan. No. 224 Group, with headquarters at Chittagong, consisted of 14 fighter and fighter-bomber squadrons made up of Hurricanes, Spitfires, Beaufighters, and Vengeances, totalling 200 aircraft. At call were the U.S.A.A.F. and R.A.F. Strategic Air Force and Brigadier-General W. D. Old's U.S.A.A.F. and R.A.F. Troop Carrier Command. During this phase of the Arakan fighting, XV Corps was reinforced by No. 3 Special Service Brigade (two, later four, commandos), 25th and 26th Indian, and British 36th Divisions, making a total of 6½ divisions.

A large engineer contingent was employed in improving communications and building airfields, whilst flotillas of small boats from the Royal Navy, the Royal Engineers, and the Service Corps supplemented the supply lines.

Opposing this formidable force was the Japanese 55th Division (Lieutenant-General T. Hanaya) and a depleted 5th Air Division (maximum 80 aircraft) which was responsible for the defence of all Burma.

The 54th Division was moving to protect the coast-line south of Akyab but took no part in the Arakan operation. Hanaya's fragile communications were by track across the Arakan Yomas to Pakokku on the Irrawaddy and from Prome by track to Taungup and thence by launch to Akyab.

New advance

During the post-monsoon months of 1943 Christison had advanced his forces methodically down the Mayu peninsula so that by mid-January 1944 he was poised to attack the heavily-fortified Japanese Maungdaw–Buthidaung line. General Gifford had ordered Slim to capture this line by mid-January, but the still-cautious Slim was behind schedule.

Meanwhile the Japanese high command, realising from the exploits of the Chindits in the previous year that neither the jungles nor the hills of Burma were impassable to determined troops, and seeing the British forces in Assam hanging down on a 300-mile-long stalk from the

▽ *Keeping a look-out on a 40-mm Bofors anti-aircraft gun on a self-propelled mounting.*

main stem on the Brahmaputra like a bunch of grapes ripe for plucking, had decided that the best means for the defence of Burma was attack. Their main plan for 1944 was to attack west over the Chindwin hills, to cut the lines of communication of IV Corps at Imphal and destroy the Allied forces in that area. As a diversion to draw away as many divisions as possible over the other side of the Arakan Yomas they would first use penetration tactics to attack and destroy the Allied forces in the Arakan. This was named the "HA-GO" offensive and was planned to start on February 3.

By that date the 5th Division, supported by tanks, was attacking the Japanese in the Tunnels area with three brigades up; the 7th Division in the Mayu valley was attacking Buthidaung, and the 81st West African Division was far away on the Kaladan river, where it achieved very little effect on the campaign apart from being a drain on the Allied air supply

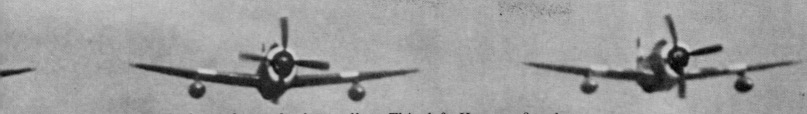

resources. Also behind these forward divisions were the 26th and 36th Divisions.

Hanaya divided his division into four. Two battalions would hold Akyab. One battalion could guard the coast of the Mayu peninsula. Two battalions ("Doi" Column) could hold the redoubts between the Mayu river and the sea which was being attacked by the six brigades (with tanks) of the 5th and 7th Divisions. He entrusted his reconnaissance regiment to screen off the West Africans in the Kala-dan valley. This left Hanaya five battalions and an engineer regiment (about 5,000 strong) for his penetration force under Major-General T. Sakurai. The rôle of the "Sakurai" Column was to pass straight through the 7th Indian Division on the night of February 3–4, seize Taung Bazar, turn left, cross the Mayu river, and cut the communications of both the 5th and 7th Divisions. Meanwhile, the "Doi" Column, manning the redoubts, would attack from the south.

All at first went well for the "Sakurai" Column. Sixteen abreast they strode along the flat paddy fields, through the heart of the 7th Division at midnight and occupied Taung Bazar 12 miles away by morning. Within an hour one battalion had crossed the Mayu river in captured boats. By noon on February 5 the whole force was behind the 5th Division and one detachment had seized Briasco Bridge on the coast road whilst the remainder overran the 5th Division's headquarters and started attacking the Administrative Area, at Sinzweya.

Here Slim's new training instructions and orders started to take effect. The Administrative Area, the capture of which the Japanese depended on for their supplies, closed up like a box. All brigades stood firm. Air supply was made available to the two forward divisions. They fought on, improvising where necessary. Gifford ordered the 36th Division to move south from Chittagong. Hanaya reinforced "Doi" Column and urged it to attack north all the harder to help Sakurai. The 7th Division cut Sakurai's tenuous lines of communication running through the area. Sakurai's code book with wireless frequencies was captured and with it his signals communication list of call signs with the result that his powers of command and control of the battles started to fail. The Administrative Box held out, all ranks of whatever arm taking part in its defence.

Christison at one point wavered, believing his 7th Division overrun, and ordered the 5th Division to move back across the Mayu range. But the more experienced Slim countermanded this order and exhorted the 26th and 36th Divisions to hasten forward to destroy the Japanese penetration forces. As long as the "Admin. Box" at Sinzweya held out, the Japanese could get no supplies and their offensive was doomed. It held from February 6 to 24, when the Ngakyedauk Pass was reopened.

The Japanese put their whole air strength into the battle and flew 350 bomber sorties. But the R.A.F. counterattacked and, although losing some transport aircraft shot down, Troop Carrier Command succeeded in delivering 2,710 tons of supplies to the Sinzweya box and the two forward divisions.

On February 24, with the approval of

The Japanese Nakajima Ki-43-II KAI Hayabusa ("Oscar") fighter

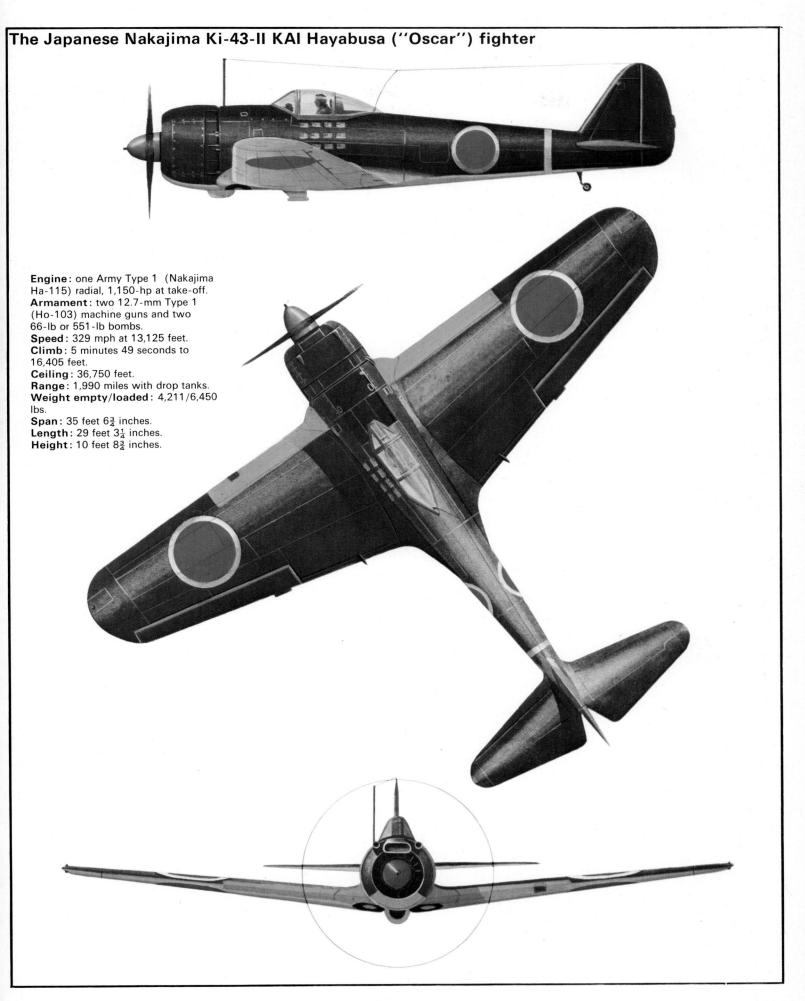

Engine: one Army Type 1 (Nakajima Ha-115) radial, 1,150-hp at take-off.
Armament: two 12.7-mm Type 1 (Ho-103) machine guns and two 66-lb or 551-lb bombs.
Speed: 329 mph at 13,125 feet.
Climb: 5 minutes 49 seconds to 16,405 feet.
Ceiling: 36,750 feet.
Range: 1,990 miles with drop tanks.
Weight empty/loaded: 4,211/6,450 lbs.
Span: 35 feet 6¾ inches.
Length: 29 feet 3¼ inches.
Height: 10 feet 8¾ inches.

2873

his army headquarters, Hanaya abandoned the "*HA-GO*" offensive. This was the end. The Japanese withdrew uneventfully. XV Corps had suffered 3,506 casualties but had held its ground, thus giving a tremendous fillip to morale throughout the army in India, an event of which the political, psychological, and propaganda sections made the maximum use.

But the Japanese in the Arakan had achieved the object given to them. One Japanese division had thrown two divisions into temporary disarray, and tied down a total 6½ divisions. The actual "*HA-GO*" offensive was carried out by about eight battalions totalling not more than 8,000 troops. Twenty-seven Indian, 18 British, seven West African, and five Gurkha battalions, accompanied by a total of 26 regiments of artillery, were brought against them. It was no fault of the Japanese soldiers that, owing to Allied technical superiority, many of these battalions and regiments could be and were quickly switched by air to the Imphal

front to restore the situation there.

Meanwhile, during the "HA-GO" offensive, the Japanese 28th Army had relieved Hanaya of responsibility for the Kaladan front and had on February 18 formed the "Koba" Force, under Colonel T. Koba, which consisted of a regimental headquarters, the 55th Reconnaissance Regiment, plus the equivalent of three infantry battalions, to face Major-General C. G. Woolner's 81st West African Division. Woolner underestimated the Japanese strength. Koba, by manoeuvre, ambush, and outflanking movement, but never by frontal attack, drove the West Africans 40 miles back from Kyauktaw and started to ooze them out of the Kaladan valley.

The attack on Imphal had now started, and Gifford wanted to transfer the 5th and 7th Divisions by air to that front as soon as possible. He allowed Christison time for the 7th Division to capture Buthidaung and 5th Division Razabil, before they were relieved by the 26th Indian and British 36th Divisions on March 22. The 25th Indian Division was also moved forward and relieved the 36th Division, which was to come under General Stilwell's command in north Burma to relieve the Chindits. Hanaya ordered all his forward units to attack and harass the British forces from all directions and

to give an impression of strength during the next four weeks, so as to hold the British in the area before he withdrew to monsoon positions. By using false identity badges and other deception methods, he made British Intelligence believe that the 54th Division had moved into the area. Koga, in the Kaladan, followed suit so successfully that the West Africans were thrown right out of the Kaladan valley and ceased to be a threat to the Japanese flank. Christison's forces, however, obtained possession of Maungdaw and the much fought over Point 551, which he thought would be a good starting line for the post-monsoon offensive.

But Gifford realised that the Arakan was a bad area in which to fight the Japanese. Having inflicted over 3,500 casualties on the British in the "HA-GO" offensive, the Japanese had caused a further 3,360 casualties in the period before the monsoon, and this excludes casualties from sickness, which were always high. So Gifford, on July 14, 1944, recommended that any idea of an offensive in Arakan in the dry season of 1944-45 should be abandoned since at least four or five divisions would appear to be necessary to achieve success. The Arakan had become a graveyard of British commanders' reputations, and a serious demoralising factor amongst their troops.

The last Arakan campaign will be dealt with in a later chapter.

◁ In one of a whole series of amphibious operations along the Burma coast, codenamed Operation "Talon", commandos wade ashore onto the Myebon peninsula from Royal Indian Navy landing craft.
Inset: Four Japanese, killed by one mortar shell.

△ *A group of Chindits, sporting the beards they were permitted to grow in the jungle. Their operations were a source of good propaganda for the British forces and the home front, who had seen the Japanese drive through the British Asian Empire in a series of apparently effortless victories.*

△ ▷ *A radio operator with his bulky and heavy equipment, which had to be carried on mules. The jungle-covered hills, with deep valleys and fierce electric storms, made signalling a difficult and exhausting job, to which was added the problem of encoding messages for security.*

▷ ▷ *Armed with the two essentials of his trade, a rifle and a spade, a Chindit soldier strides through the jungle. His battered bush hat betrays the multitude of uses to which it has been put, keeping off sun and rain, and acting as a pillow at night.*

CHAPTER 172
Wingate's Dream: the 1st Chindit operation

In January 1942, when the Japanese invaded Burma, the British War Office offered General Wavell, Commander-in-Chief India, the services of Lieutenant-Colonel Orde Wingate, D.S.O. and bar, who had previously carried out guerrilla operations in Palestine and Abyssinia with conspicuous success. Wavell, under whom Wingate had served, recognised his excellent if unorthodox qualities, saw a role for him in Burma, and accepted this offer.

On Wingate's arrival in India after the fall of Rangoon, Wavell sent him to carry out a reconnaissance in north Burma, which he thought might be suitable terrain for guerrillas. Wingate flew in and was conducted around north Burma by the commandant of the Bush Warfare School at Maymyo, Major J. M. Calvert, who was later to join him. Calvert also motored Wingate south some hundreds of miles to Prome to meet Lieutenant-General Slim, commander of I Burma Corps. This corps had only just been formed, after the fall of Rangoon.

After a detailed reconnaissance and after discussing the matter with many people, including Chiang Kai-shek in Chungking, Wingate returned to India.

He reported to Wavell that at that juncture there were neither time nor troops available to form a pattern of guerrilla warfare in north Burma, but he did recommend forming and training a special force of brigade strength, which could penetrate behind the Japanese forces and destroy their communications and perhaps manoeuvre them out of the area.

The first Chindits

This experimental force became the 77th Indian Infantry Brigade, made up of the 13th King's (Liverpool) Regiment; 3rd/2nd Gurkha Rifles; British 142nd Commando Company; a Burma Rifle battalion, which was split into detachments amongst each column; as well as skilled signal and R.A.F. sections attached to each column. In addition there was a small tactical Brigade Headquarters which General Wingate took into the field. Behind this, in the rear areas, was a supply organisation which remained at base and which looked after all the administrative and supply arrangements of the columns in the field. This rear headquarters looked large to those who saw it in India. But it must be remembered that all those who would normally be attached to a battalion to look after its administration and would normally accompany it into battle, were extracted from the columns in the field and carried out their supply and administrative duties from a distance through the medium of aircraft and radio.

Rigorous training

This force was trained most rigorously by Wingate in the sparse jungles of the Central Provinces. The men forming the force had nothing very special about them. There was a small nucleus of officers and men from the Bush Warfare School in Maymyo, which in itself was a cover name for a special mission to China. But apart from these men and a draft from the Commandos in the Middle East, which helped form No. 142 Commando (which never numbered more than 100 men), the remainder of the infantry forming this brigade came from second or third line troops who had not had much training. The Burma Rifles turned out to be very good in reconnaissance and in their

knowledge of the country, which helped the column forward. Their officers, largely ex-forestry officers, were excellent. Most of the officers and other ranks of the battalion were not picked men and it is all to their credit that they did so well. The fact that they were not picked men made all other units in the Burma Army realise after the operation that if these men could do it, they too could do it.

Wingate himself trained cadres of officers and N.C.O.s in every little detail of column and bivouac life, including quick reaction to alarm and taking offensive action. He taught men how to cook in the jungle, the use of machine guns, mortars, camouflage, navigation through the jungle, how to look after mules, how to cross rivers, and so on. He himself was tireless in his attention to detail. He then expected his officers to follow his example and teach their men.

He stressed that total reliance was to be placed on mulepack transport for all weapons, ammunition, signals, and medical supplies, supplemented by direct air supply to each column in the field at the request of the R.A.F. officers accompanying the column. Mules would feed on bamboo shoots collected by the mule leaders and augmented by grain, free dropped from the air. Wingate made up a ration of nuts, raisins, biscuits, tea, salt, and sugar, which was to be augmented by the purchase of rice and buffalo meat whenever possible.

Calvert's adjutant at the Bush Warfare School, Major Peter Lord, who had once been secretary of the International Club at Tientsin, set up and organised the

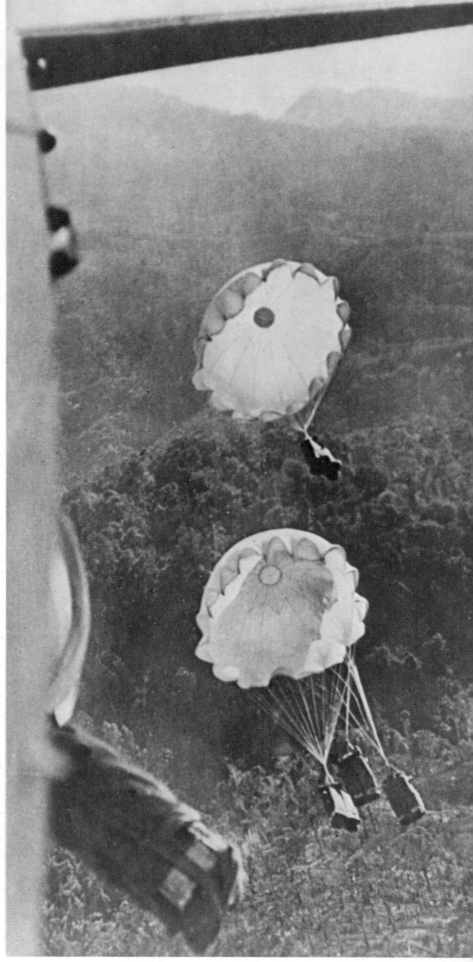

whole air supply system, assisted and advised by Squadron-Leader Longmore and Squadron-Leader R. Thompson.

This force was named the "Chindits", which was an anglicised version of the name of the mythical griffon, the "Chinthe", the protector of the Burma pagodas.

The first Chindit operation

Originally the raid planned for the seven Chindit columns, each of about 400 men and 100 mules with two 3-inch mortars and two medium machine guns, was to be supported by a general offensive by IV Corps from Imphal. But IV Corps' (Scoones) communications were not ready, and so it was reluctant to advance across the Chindwin in any strength. Wavell, however, was determined that this experimental brigade should test out not only the Japanese but these new means of operating in the deep jungle. Wavell came forward to Imphal, inspected the 77th Brigade and, after deep thought, directed it into the attack alone. Wavell

had had to consider whether the risk of losing all or part of this brigade on a mission of little strategic value, in order to attempt to burst the bubble of Japanese invincibility, would be balanced by the experience gained and the loss of technical surprise when such tactics had to be used later to support a general offensive. He wisely understood the overwhelming importance of morale (compared with mere numbers of troops in such a terrain, weapons, and possession of territory) and felt certain that such an expedition under such a leader was the sure way of restoring the flagging morale of the army in India.

Wavell wanted Wingate to be an irritant to arouse his generals out of their mood of apathy and despair.

Into action

On February 14 the headquarters and three British and four Gurkha columns of the 77th Brigade successfully crossed the Chindwin and advanced secretly on a broad front through the jungle-covered

△ ◁ *A supply drop in progress. The lessons learned about re-supply from the air were acted upon during the second Chindit expedition in 1944.*

◁ ◁ *A dispatcher's view of a supply drop. Some unbreakable stores were dropped without parachutes, and while this saved silk and parachute cord, it could be dangerous for the collecting party. Some men suffered serious injuries when they were hit by free-falling panniers, and in one disastrous drop the bottom came out of a bag of 5,000 rupees.*

△ *Chindits move off the track for a break during the march. Japanese search parties worked up the waterways when they were looking for Chindit bivouacs, so the latter took care not to camp close to streams.*

△ *Lance-Corporal James Rogerson, a Gurkha private, and Private Jack Wilson after their tour behind the enemy lines. The men carried a 72-pound pack, which included seven days' rations, a rifle and bayonet, a* dah *or* kukri *(machete or Gurkha knife), three grenades, groundsheet, spare shirt and trousers, four spare pairs of socks, balaclava helmet, jack-knife, rubber shoes, housewife, toggle-rope, canvas life-jacket, mess tin, ration-bags, water bottle, and a* chagal *(canvas water bottle), besides other items of personal kit. Blankets and Bren guns were carried by mules.*

hills into central Burma. Their objective was the main north-south Burma railway between Mandalay and Mogaung. The distance from their starting point to the railway direct was about 140 miles. Major Dunlop's No. 1 (Gurkha) Column was the first to reach the railway on March 3 when it destroyed railway bridges near Kyaikthin. No. 3 (Gurkha) Column (Calvert) did the same 40 miles north at Nankan on the night March 5-6. No. 5 (King's) Column (Fergusson) on the same night brought down an avalanche of rock onto the railway in the Bongyaung (Bonchaung) Gorge. The forces taking part in this operation totalled about 3,000 men and 800 mules.

The Japanese 18th and 33rd divisions of the 15th Army, under Lieutenant-General Iida, were the formations most affected by this raid, and for a while they were bewildered by it. They did not take the situation seriously until Dunlop (Royal Scots) blew the railway on March 3. Then Iida ordered three regiments, each of three battalions, to round up the raiders.

Wingate, however, exalted by this first success, ordered his columns to cross the 1,000-yard wide Irrawaddy. He envisaged

forming a base in the friendly Kachin Hills to the north-east, from where he could operate with his back to the Chinese during the next few months. But he also ordered Calvert and Fergusson to attack the Burma Road in the Maymyo area, where the Japanese headquarters were situated and therefore where the maximum reaction to the raid would result.

First defeat

But one of the Gurkha columns had already met with disaster when approaching the railway, and had been dispersed. The news of this spread to the other Gurkha columns and it became more difficult to keep up their morale. It should be explained that whilst the Gurkhas, when properly trained and with officers who speak their language, are magnificent troops, they naturally cannot so easily change the tactics and methods taught them at their depots at short notice as can, for example, British troops, who understood the language in which the new concepts of such tactics are aught. The Gurkha battalion given to Wingate for this operation was woefully short of experienced officers and men, and only about one officer in each column spoke Gurkhali well. In Calvert's column, for instance, only one British officer with the Gurkha company was over the age of 19. It is all the more remarkable that these young officers led their fine young men, assisted by excellent Gurkhali warrant officers and N.C.O.s, through nearly three months of operations in the jungle without cracking.

The crossing of the Irrawaddy was not easy and more than one column was attacked whilst carrying out this difficult manoeuvre. Perhaps the crossing was a mistake. After their initial rapid march and successful demolitions, the Chindits found themselves hemmed in between the Irrawaddy and the Shweli rivers in a dry inhospitable area with no nearby targets to attack and at the extreme range of their wireless sets and air supply communications. The Japanese used regiments from three (18th, 33rd, 56th) of their four divisions in Burma at that time to try to surround and destroy the Chindits.

Many small actions were fought until the time came when Wingate, after radio consultation with IV Corps, decided to withdraw his force. He ordered his column commanders to try to bring back their columns complete into India or to take them on to China. He gave them the alternative option of splitting into dispersal groups as taught in training, so that they might infiltrate between the strands of the Japanese net which was now surrounding them. One King's column (Gilkes) chose the longer, more arduous, but safer route to China. Another King's column, under Scott, who had been a Royal Engineer, chose to make an airstrip in an open space in the jungle and be flown out from the other side of the Irrawaddy. The remainder recrossed the Irrawaddy either in dispersal groups or columns and made their way back to the Chindwin. Unfortunately many of them thought they were safe on reaching the Chindwin, but IV Corps had withdrawn from it and the Japanese were now using it as a stop line to catch the Chindit columns in that area. The result was that many prisoners were taken on the Chindwin itself, when the dispersal group thought that it had reached safe harbour and had relaxed.

Of the 3,000 men and 800 mules which

△ *Major Bernard Fergusson, Black Watch, who led Number 5 Column. In 1944 Stilwell described him in a letter of introduction, "Help this man, he looks like a dude, but I think he's a soldier." "On the whole I liked it," commented Fergusson.*
▽ *The first Chindit expedition.*

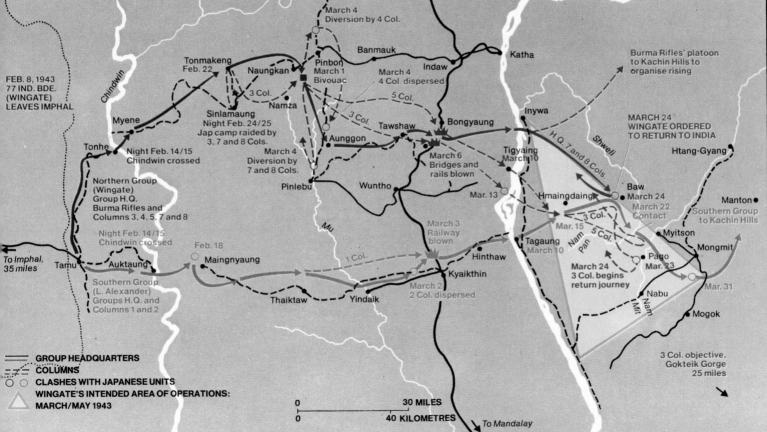

FEB. 8, 1943
77 IND. BDE.
(WINGATE)
LEAVES IMPHAL

March 4
Diversion by 4 Col.

Irrawaddy

Banmauk   Katha

Burma Rifles' platoon
to Kachin Hills to
organise rising

Tonmakeng
Feb. 22

Naungkan

Pinbon
March 1
Bivouac

March 4
4 Col. dispersed

Indaw

Inywa

MARCH 24
WINGATE ORDERED
TO RETURN TO INDIA

Htang-Gyang

Chindwin

Myene

3 Col.

Namza

5 Col.

Sinlamaung
Night Feb. 24/25
Jap camp raided by
3, 7 and 8 Cols.

3 Col.

Tawshaw

Bongyaung

Tigyaing
March 10

H.Q. 7 and 8 Cols.

Shweli

Tonhe

Night Feb. 14/15
Chindwin crossed

March 4
Diversion by
7 and 8 Cols.

Aunggon

March 6
Bridges and
rails blown

Baw
March 24

Manton

Southern Group
to Kachin Hills

Northern Group
(Wingate)
Group H.Q.
Burma Rifles and
Columns 3, 4, 5, 7 and 8

Pinlebu

Wuntho

Mar. 13

Hmaingdaing

3 Col.

Myitson

Mongmit

Night Feb. 14/15
Chindwin crossed

Feb. 18

Mu

March 3
Railway
blown

Mar. 15

5 Col.

Pago
Mar. 23

Mar. 31

To Imphal,
35 miles

Tamu

Auktaung

Maingnyaung

1 Col.

Tagaung
March 10

Hinthaw

Nam Pan

March 24
3 Col. begins
return journey

Nabu

Southern Group
(L. Alexander)
Groups H.Q. and
Columns 1 and 2

Thaiktaw

Yindaik

Kyaikthin

March 2
2 Col. dispersed

March 22
Contact

Nam Mit

Mogok

GROUP HEADQUARTERS
COLUMNS
CLASHES WITH JAPANESE UNITS
WINGATE'S INTENDED AREA OF OPERATIONS:
MARCH/MAY 1943

3 Col. objective,
Gokteik Gorge
25 miles

0   30 MILES
0   40 KILOMETRES

To Mandalay

had crossed the Chindwin, about 2,182 men and two mules returned, having covered between 1,000 and 1,500 miles in enemy-dominated territory. The remainder had been killed, captured, or if mules, eaten. But those who returned, although suffering from malaria, dysentery, jungle sores, and malnutrition, were in high spirits and proud of their achievement. Sent on leave and supported by a well-directed public relations campaign in the press, they had a startling effect on the raising of morale of all ranks throughout India, especially at that time when the defeats in the Arakan had further depressed men's minds. There they were, ordinary second line battalions and any-

thing but picked troops, but they had gone through Burma and "singed Tojo's moustache". So their comrades in units throughout India and Assam said "if that lot can run rings round the Japanese we can do better".

Japanese conclusions

However, there was another unexpected reaction. General Mutaguchi, a man of strong personality who had been uniformly successful in battle since 1937, and who was the acknowledged "victor of Singapore", was commanding the 18th

Division during the Chindit operation. He had studied Wingate's tactics and use of ground closely and came to admire his methods. So when he was promoted to command of the 15th Army he wanted to emulate Wingate's methods and to improve on them. Initially he arranged a discussion group on the results of the first Wingate operation. He then ordered a reconnaissance to be made over the Chindwin and proposed a Chindit-type operation for the 1944 season against Imphal and Kohima, but on a much greater scale, with a force totalling three divisions relying mainly on pack transport. War games were held to test out his ideas and, with some misgivings, especi-

ally from the Japanese Army Air Force, Imperial General Headquarters in Tokyo agreed with Mutaguchi's plan – with the proviso that it should be linked with a campaign by the newly formed Indian National Army to instigate an insurrection in India, coupled with other subversive activities.

Imphal idea born

Thus the first Chindit operation was the direct begetter of Mutaguchi's "U-GO" offensive against the 14th Army at Imphal in March 1944. This operation, after

▽ ◁ ◁ *A party of Chindits carrying wounded on an extemporised stretcher.*
▽ ◁ *A rigger and radio operator greeted by Major Walter P. Scott at an airfield in Burma.*
▽ *Rubber assault boats used during the march into Burma. The Chindwin, and other rivers which flow from northern Burma to the sea and divide the country in half, were a major natural obstacle. For the Japanese they also served as a stop line on to which they could drive some of the small parties of Chindits when the columns had broken up.*

△ One of six officers and men of the King's Regiment on the first expedition in 1943 is decorated by Lord Wavell, Viceroy of India. Fergusson admitted that the Chindits had not achieved a great deal, though they had distracted the Japanese from some operations. However, they had "amassed experience on which a future has already begun to be built". Wingate went home and captured the imagination of both Churchill and Roosevelt.

effort should be put into offensive operations to achieve this object."

In order to achieve this result the British Chiefs-of-Staff decided to form six Long Range Penetration Groups (L.R.P.G.), which would conduct operations as outlined by Brigadier Wingate and enable the Allies to seize sufficient of north Burma to open a road to China.

These six L.R.P. brigades would each consist of four battalions and attached troops. The force, which was known variously as the Special Force, the 3rd Indian Infantry Division (as a cover name), or the Chindits, would consist of two Indian infantry brigades (77th and 111th) already in being; three brigades formed from the battle-experienced British 70th Division; and one brigade formed from the 81st West African Division. The three battalions of this African brigade would be available to this force to act as garrisons for the air bases formed in the jungle to support each brigade.

These bases, which Wingate called "strongholds", were what the modern tactician tends to call "pivots of manoeuvre".

To support China

At the "Sextant" Conference held in Cairo in November 1943, which Chiang Kai-shek attended, the Combined Chiefs-of-Staff ordered "the occupation of Upper Burma by the Allies to start in February 1944 in order to improve (a) the air and (b) the land routes to China. What was attempted elsewhere in Asia would be in support of this main effort."

The main reason for the Allies giving this plan of operations top priority was the real fear that, unless the British and Americans opened up even such tenuous communications to China in the manner projected, China would drop out of the war and thus allow the 26 Japanese divisions operating in China to be used elsewhere against the Allies. It is important that this agreed plan of action by the Allies should be borne in mind throughout all discussions on this campaign, because future operations by either side as the battlefield spread, tended to blur the horizon and deflect certain commanders' minds away from the maintenance of this objective which had been laid down by the inter-Allied high command.

achieving initial success, failed because Mutaguchi had apparently not understood that the vital necessity for such an operation was dominance of the air, and consequent reliable air supply and close air support in lieu of artillery.

Much has been made of the divergencies of opinion amongst the Allies on how they should conduct the war against Japan, but one decision made in 1943 stands out plainly. At the Combined Chiefs-of-Staff "Quadrant" Conference in Quebec in August 1943, which Brigadier Wingate attended at Churchill's request, it was decided "To carry out operations for the capture of upper Burma in order to improve the air route and establish overland communications with China. Our main

the 2nd Chindit Operation

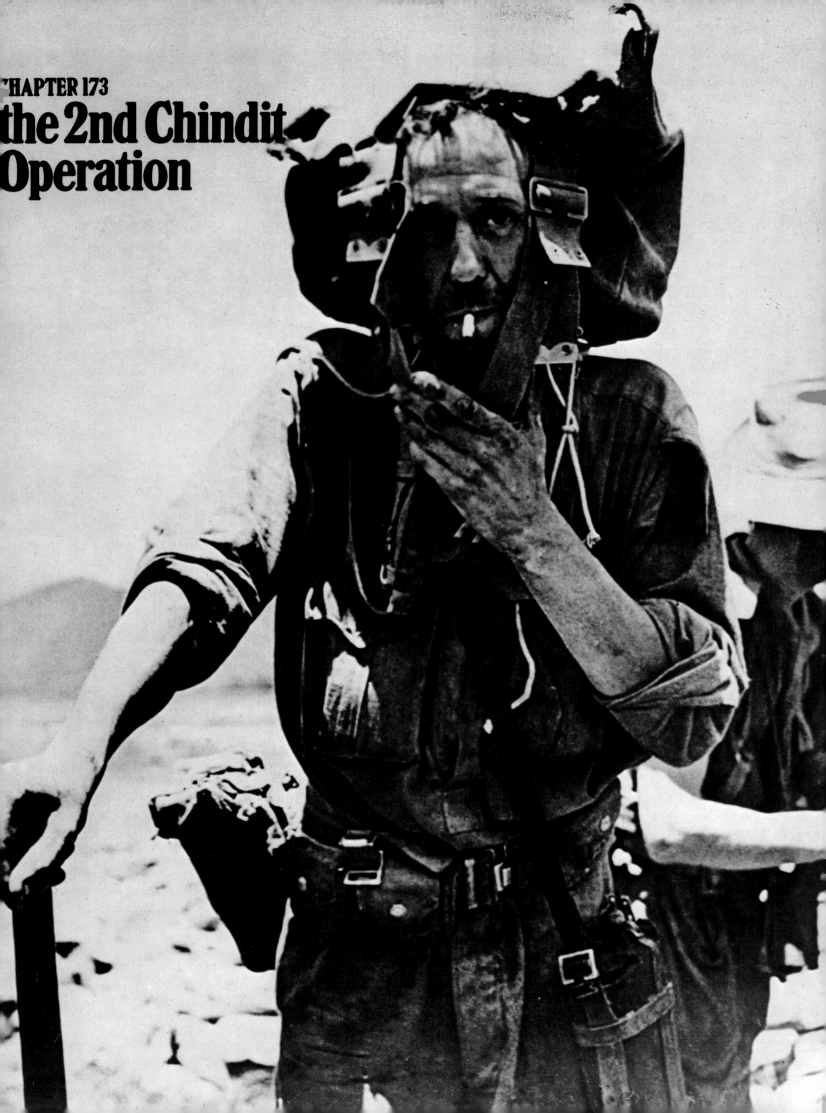

△ *General Orde Wingate and Colonel Phil Cochran, U.S.A.A.F., brief American pilots. The air support for the second Chindit expedition, in both attack and support operations, was prompt, efficient, and plentiful.*
Previous page: *With his large pack as a hat, a soldier pauses in the harsh sunlight to enjoy a cigarette.*

The four battalions in each L.R.P. brigade were split into and trained to move in eight columns of about 400 men each, comprising a four-platoon infantry company with two 3-inch mortars and two medium machine gun detachments, and supported by R.A.F., sapper, signaller, and medical detachments, all of which were based on mule transport and air supply. Each column had about 56 mules (much less than in the first operation as reliance on air supply was far greater) and each mule leader was interchangeable with men in the infantry company (and *vice versa*), thereby providing a source of reinforcement. The very important R.A.F. detachment, led by an active pilot officer, who had already flown in action in Burma, was responsible for the direction of close air support in lieu of artillery, air supply, and the air evacuation of the wounded. In those conditions and at that period of army/air liaison, it was considered preferable by the men on the ground to have nine officers piloting aircraft supporting them in the air and nine experienced officers on the ground who spoke the same language directing the pilots in the air, rather than 27 pilots in the air with no one on the ground in whom they had faith and confidence. These R.A.F. detachments uniformly proved themselves of a very high standard and,

besides the execution of their duties, did much to maintain the morale and offensive spirit of all ranks in the columns to which they were attached.

The column formations were designed for movement through the jungle, for cutting communications, and for the general harassment of the rear areas of the Japanese forces facing the British, American, and Chinese forces. But General Wingate felt that such a tough and seasoned enemy would not react sufficiently or withdraw his forces just because of this harassment alone. The Japanese would not just allow themselves to be manoeuvred out of a position without a fight. Therefore he emphasised to brigade commanders that these columns should be instructed and rehearsed in reforming into battalions and into brigades under their commanders, and thus be able to fight pitched battles of long duration in order to seize worthwhile targets or to destroy a sizable force sent against them. When that occurred, artillery and other essential support units would be flown in to convert the brigade into a hard-hitting formation. When that particular objective was overcome, Wingate envisaged more orthodox garrison units being flown in to hold that objective and the L.R.P. brigades dispersing again into columns in order to prepare the way for another attack. They would leave the artillery which had been flown into them to support the garrison troops they had left behind.

Essential to the success of such operations was a base for each brigade in the jungle, centred around a fairweather airfield and garrisoned by one static and one mobile floater column. The floater column was designed to attack the enemy's rear when the latter assaulted the air base. Wingate, a gunner, believed in flying in sufficient calibre of artillery for the defence of the base to overcome and outgun anything the enemy could bring to bear overland in that terrain. Anti-aircraft artillery and a squadron or flight of aircraft might also be flown in so that they could, with radar coverage, help defend the base and also provide support to the brigades in the field. From these forward bases light aircraft would operate to the columns to evacuate the wounded who would otherwise encumber them, and bring in specialist reinforcements and generally act in liaison. From these bases transport aircraft would each night move the wounded in bulk to hospital in India.

Thus a man could be wounded in battle during the day and find himself in a comfortable base hospital the same night.

It must be emphasised that it was never intended that these well-trained, well-armed columns would merely act in a pin-pricking guerrilla, harassing, rôle, but would only do so temporarily, in order to produce a situation of which they could then take advantage by re-forming into a hard-hitting brigade and overcoming a contingent of the enemy. Tito in Yugoslavia, the Russian and Ukrainian partisans in 1944, and occasionally Mao Tse-tung's forces operated on similar lines, but the greatest and most successful exponent of this theory of operations since Wingate, although without air supply, has been General Giap in Vietnam.

It was unfortunate that in the months before the campaign started Wingate was struck down by typhus, and he did not have sufficient time to train and inculcate his ideas deeply into the minds of some of his brigade commanders, so that a few of them never fully understood how Wingate wanted them to operate. This was not their fault, but it did affect operations later.

General Marshall also sent an American brigade, later known as Merrill's Marauders or "Galahad" Force, to train and operate with Wingate. But later General Stilwell found it was essential to have some American troops in the field to help his Chinese divisions forward, so Wingate lost the use of this fine force.

Wingate wanted six L.R.P. groups in order to ensure that there was a maximum of three of them operating whilst the others recuperated and then became available for relief. He estimated that an L.R.P. brigade could not continue to operate at its best advantage after it had been in the jungle behind the lines for more than about two months. But, as so often occurs in war, once the major forces of both sides are committed, all the reserves of both sides (including all the L.R.P. brigades) were also committed to battle.

General Arnold, commanding the U.S. Army Air Forces, also allotted No. 1 Air Commando, under Colonel P. Cochran, to the theatre with the primary task of assisting Wingate's Chindits in their operations. This force consisted of 13 Dakotas (C-47), 225 Waco gliders, 100 Stinson L-5 light aircraft, a squadron of 12 Mitchell medium bombers (B-25), 30 Mustang fighter-bombers (P-51) and six experimental helicopters.

These air commandos were designed by

◁ *Lord Louis Mountbatten with Cochran. Despite his natural charm, Cochran was a firm leader. His Air Commando served as flying artillery, logistic link, and ambulance service. The L-1's and L-5's of the Light Plane Force ferried wounded men to base hospitals, and the courage of their pilots earned the lasting respect of the men on the ground.*

▽ *Lieutenant-Colonel Walter Scott, Brigadier J. M. Calvert, and Colonel John Alison, U.S.A.A.F., before the take-off for "Broadway" on the night of March 6-7, 1944.*

The American Waco CG-4A transport glider

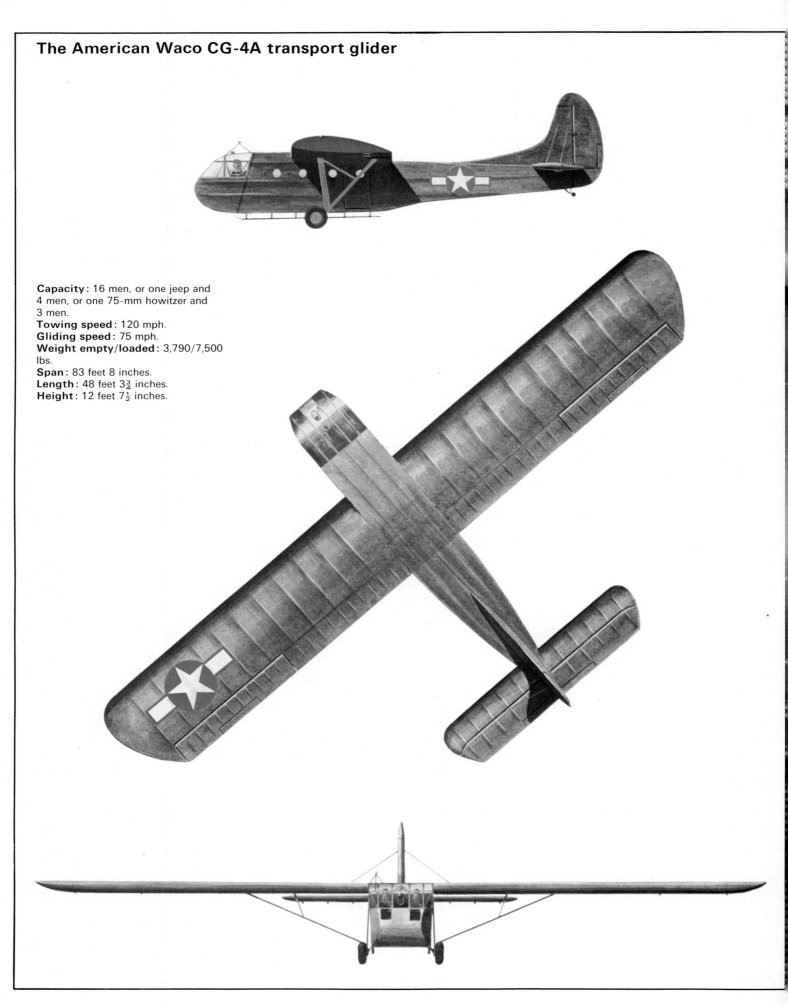

Capacity: 16 men, or one jeep and 4 men, or one 75-mm howitzer and 3 men.
Towing speed: 120 mph.
Gliding speed: 75 mph.
Weight empty/loaded: 3,790/7,500 lbs.
Span: 83 feet 8 inches.
Length: 48 feet 3¾ inches.
Height: 12 feet 7½ inches.

General Arnold to pep up and put life into flagging campaigns which were becoming moribund, using the high morale and a higher grade of officer and man which air forces attracted, coupled with first class technical support, to act as a blood transfusion for "anaemic" troops on the ground, who through casualties had lost their attacking spirit.

The Americans had already strongly recommended that Wingate should be made Supreme Commander in South-East Asia, but were willing to bow to the British objections when the latter produced Lord Louis Mountbatten as an alternative.

Balance of forces

The Japanese had eight divisions, one (24th) Independent Mixed Brigade, one I.N.A. (Indian National Army) brigade, and one (5th) Air Division, with one division (53rd) on its way from Formosa. This force was split up into three armies (15th, 28th, 33rd), under the Burma Area Army commander (Lieutenant-General M. Kawabe) at Maymyo. The 33rd Army (Lieutenant-General M. Honda) held the northern and eastern front with the 18th Division facing Stilwell's forces on the Ledo Road, and 56th Division opposing "Yoke" Force on the Salween.

The 25th Army's (Lieutenant-General Sakurai) responsibility stretched along the coast from Akyab to Bassein in the Malay peninsula, with the 55th Division opposing XV Corps. The 54th Division was responsible for the coastline south of Akyab to Taungup, including Ramree Island. The 2nd Division covered the Irrawaddy delta and the coastline to the Malayan border.

The 15th Army (Lieutenant-General R. Mutaguchi: 15th, 31st, and 33rd Divisions) was preparing to launch its three-pronged "U-GO" offensive against IV Corps at Imphal and Kohima. Mutaguchi also had under his command the I.N.A. brigade for the exploitation of any revolt occurring in Bengal. He was relying on the 53rd Division, now on its way from Formosa via the Burma-Siam railway, to act as his reserve, although this division had never been assigned to him.

However, General Kawabe was to divert this division against Wingate's airborne attack. His only other reserve were the four battalions (139th, 140th, 141st, 142nd) of the 24th Independent Mixed Brigade (Major-General Hyashi), which were stretched out in an anti-airborne rôle along the railway from Tenasserim to Mandalay.

The 5th Air Division consisted of about 200 aircraft, including five fighter regiments (100 aircraft), two light bomber and two reconnaissance regiments (60 aircraft), and two heavy bomber regiments (30 aircraft).

The Burma-Siam Railway had been opened on October 23, 1943, so that there was now a rail link from Rangoon to Bangkok. From Bangkok the Japanese supply lines stretched another 3,000 sea miles to Japan, across the U.S. submarine-infested South China Sea. Within Burma, Kawabe had the advantage of interior lines of communication and could, if not interrupted by airborne forces, quickly move units from one front to another. Mutaguchi had built up a five-day dump of ammunition and supplies at Indaw to support his offensive.

Against this total of nine divisions, two independent brigades, and one air division, the Allies' main superiority was in the air, in tanks (if they could be applied), and in numbers, but not in homogeneity. The Japanese units had had much greater battle experience than the British and Indian ones, and had recently been brought up to strength with reinforcements, but the new divisions such as the 53rd were mainly made up of older reservists and were not of the same calibre as, for instance, the 18th and 33rd Divisions.

The Allied ground forces consisted of 15 divisions (nine Indian, two British, one West African, one East African, and three Chinese) plus the 12 ill-equipped Chinese divisions of "Yoke" Force on the Salween front. Besides these formed divisions there were two tank brigades (50th and 254th), six long-range penetration brigades of four battalions each (including Merrill's U.S. Marauders), one parachute brigade, and one commando brigade. There were also locally raised forces in the mountains, such as the Lushai Brigade south of Imphal and the Tripura Rifles in the Arakan Yomas. A second West African Division (82nd) was completing its training in India.

It should be pointed out that initially each brigade in an Indian division had one British and two Indian or Gurkha battalions. Also, when war broke out, the divisional and corps artillery was British

Born in 1903, **Orde Wingate** established a reputation as an original military thinker early in the war. Between January and late May 1941 he led guerrilla groups known as "Gideon Force" in Abyssinia. As the assistant to Emperor Haile Selassie and his nationalist forces he employed tactics which led to the evacuation of a large number of positions by the Italians and the capture of many prisoners. In May 1942 he went to Burma and inspected the ground before the British retreat. The following year in February, eight groups of Chindits, men trained in long range penetration and supplied by aircraft, crossed the River Chindwin into occupied Burma. Until June they harassed Japanese communications, and when the survivors returned they showed that this type of operation was completely feasible. The publicity caught Churchill's attention and the second Chindit operation in 1944 had full air support. Two brigades were flown in and a third marched. Japanese attacks on the force and its assaults on enemy communications did much to break the main offensive by the Japanese against the British in India. On March 24 Wingate was killed when his aircraft flew into a mountain in Assam. He was a man who had dedicated friends, but also some prejudiced critics. Of Wingate, Churchill said "He was a man of genius who might well have become a man of destiny."

He twice refused promotion to lieutenant-general.

▽ *In a flurry of spray a Waco CG-4A glider lands in a wet paddy field at "Broadway".*
▽ ◁ ◁ *A line up of Wacos before take-off.*
▽ ◁ *A glider is towed into position.*
▽ ▽ *The end of the journey; a Waco makes a dry landing at "Broadway". A consortium of 16 manufacturing plants built a total of 13,909 of these gliders during the war years.*

but the artillery was in process of being "Indianised". The engineers in the Indian divisions were all sappers and miners drawn from Madras, Bombay, and Bengal.

These units at the beginning of March were distributed amongst:

1. XV Corps (Christison), consisting of the 5th, 7th, 25th, and 26th Indian Divisions, the British 36th Division, the 81st West African Division, the 3rd Special Service (Commando) Brigade;

2. IV Corps (Scoones), consisting of the 17th, 20th, and 23rd Indian Divisions and the 254th Indian Tank Brigade;

3. XXXIII Corps (Stopford), the Command Reserve, consisting of the British 2nd Division, the 19th Indian Division, the 50th Tank Brigade, and the 50th Indian Parachute Brigade;

4. Special Force "The Chindits" (Major-General Orde Wingate) (Mountbatten had offered to promote Wingate to Lieutenant-General but he had refused, asking that it might be granted when his force had achieved success.);

5. Northern Combat Area Command (Stilwell), consisting of the 2nd, 30th, and 38th Chinese Divisions, and the 5307th Composite Unit (Provisional), or, as it was more commonly known, Merrill's Marauders; and

6. Theatre Reserve, consisting of the 11th East African Division and the 99th Indian Brigade, both in Ceylon, and the 82nd West African Division, in India.

The Chindit Force was composed of six brigades, the first three of which had been constituted from the 70th Division, an experienced formation which had seen active service in the Western Desert and

at Tobruk:

a. 14th Infantry Brigade (Brigadier T. Brodie), consisting of the 1st Bedfordshire and Hertfordshire Regiment, the 7th Leicestershire Regiment, the 2nd Black Watch, and the 2nd York and Lancaster Regiment;

b. 16th Infantry Brigade (Brigadier B. E. Fergusson), consisting of 51st/69th Field Regiment, Royal Artillery, the 2nd Queen's Royal Regiment; the 2nd Leicestershire Regiment; and the 45th Reconnaissance Regiment;

c. 23rd Infantry Brigade (Brigadier L. E. C. Perowne), consisting of the 60th Field Regiment, R.A., the 2nd Duke of Wellington's Regiment, the 4th Border Regiment, and the 1st Essex Regiment;

d. 77th Indian Infantry Brigade (Brigadier J. M. Calvert), consisting of the 1st King's (Liverpool) Regiment, the 1st Lancashire Fusiliers, the 1st South Staffordshire Regiment, the 3/6th Gurkha Rifles, and the 3/9th Gurkha Rifles;

e. 111st Indian Infantry Brigade (Brigadier W. D. A. Lentaigne), consisting of the 2nd King's Own Royal Regiment, the 1st Cameronians, the 3/4th Gurkha Rifles, and the 4/9th Gurkha Rifles; and the

f. 3rd West African Brigade (Brigadier A. H. Gillmore), consisting of the 6th Nigeria Regiment, the 7th Nigeria Regiment, and the 12th Nigeria Regiment.

Each brigade was allocated one company of British/Indian or West African engineers, a detachment of Burma Rifles, medical and R.A.F. detachments, plus troops of field (25-pounder) or light A.A. (Bofors) artillery from H.Q. Special Force as the circumstances required.

Whilst the Japanese relied on interior lines of communication, mostly emanating from the Irrawaddy valley, the Allied forces were distributed in four quite distinct geographical zones, separated from each other by major physical features along a 2,000-mile reach of mountains. It was only by making use of the third dimension of air power that these four thrusts could be co-ordinated and reinforcements sent from one zone to another. A fifth thrust from the air (a fifth column), cutting the Japanese lines of communication and thus isolating each of their battlefields, would allow the Allies to advance over the major obstacles confronting them into the Burma plain and the dry open zone where their *matériel* superiority in tanks, artillery, and aircraft could be applied most effectively.

As noted already, in March 1944 the Japanese had at most 200 operational aircraft in Burma. The Allies, on the other hand, had a minimum of 1,200 aircraft (including reserves, but excluding those employed in supplying China over the "Hump"). This is calculated on the low figure of 15 aircraft per squadron. The Allied air forces were divided into six parts:

1. 3rd Tactical Air Force, consisting of 26 R.A.F. and seven U.S.A.A.F. fighter and fighter-bomber squadrons;

2. Strategic Air Force, consisting of three R.A.F. and eight U.S.A.A.F. medium and heavy bomber squadrons;

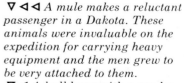

◁ *A glider on single tow by a C-47 Dakota over the 8,000-foot high Assam Hills. The maximum towing speed was 120 m.p.h.; and though there were some accidents when tow lines parted, the scattered gliders served to confuse the Japanese about the British intentions.*

▽ ◁ ◁ *A mule makes a reluctant passenger in a Dakota. These animals were invaluable on the expedition for carrying heavy equipment and the men grew to be very attached to them.*
▽ ◁ *A bulldozer with a grader levels the landing ground at "Broadway".*
▽ *Before the heavy equipment arrived, troops levelled the paddy fields for the airstrip. Squadron-Leader R. "Bobby" Thompson, the R.A.F. liaison officer, sent back a message to Cochran as the Dakotas began to land, "La Guardia has nothing on us. Can take over 100 a night."*

3. Troop Carrier Command, consisting of four R.A.F. and two U.S.A.A.F. Dakota squadrons, with the exception of one R.A.F. squadron flying Hudsons);
4. Three R.A.F. and three U.S.A.A.F. photographic reconnaissance squadrons;
5. Reserves, consisting of seven R.A.F. fighter and five R.A.F. and Royal Netherlands Air Force Catalina flying boat squadrons; and
6. Non-operational squadrons, including 14 R.A.F. and Royal Indian Air Force and six U.S.A.A.F. ones.

This gave the Allies a total of 67 operational and 20 non-operational squadrons.

The Chindit airborne assault

The main object of the Chindit operation in March 1944, as laid down in the "Quadrant" and "Sextant" Conferences, was to cut the lines of communications to the Japanese forces facing Stilwell's advance down the Ledo Road and so assist his capture of Mogaung and Myitkyina, plus a belt of territory stretching at least 50 miles further south so that his eventual hold on these two towns would be secure.

The original method designed by Wingate was to pass one L.R.P. brigade (the 16th under Fergusson) in by land and two (the 77th and 111th) by air to capture the communication centre and airfield of Indaw. Wingate then wanted the Allies to land an Indian division at Indaw to hold the airfield whilst the three brigades used Indaw as a base and a pivot of manoeuvre to harass the Japanese communications emanating out of that centre. Wingate hoped that when these original three brigades had operated for two or three months, which he considered was the limit of their operational ability, he could relieve them by his other three brigades which still required further training. However Mountbatten could not promise that such a division could be made available to hold Indaw. In fact the 3rd West African Brigade was allotted to Wingate as an alternative for this airfield protection duty. Wingate felt that once his forces were "in the guts of the enemy", as he put it, he could then play it by ear, and besides cutting the Japanese 18th Division's communications he could also spare columns to do the same to the

◁◁ *A Gurkha column moves off*
into the jungle . . .
◁ *. . . and pulls off the track to*
ake a break.

▲ *A mule loaded with bulky and*
heavy equipment.
▽ *A Japanese truck ambushed*
by the 7th Nigeria Regiment
near Sepein. The Nigerians came
new to the campaign and their
enthusiasm and willingness to
learn was a tonic to the Chindits.

Japanese communications feeding the divisions opposite IV Corps.

The 16th Brigade started its arduous 360-mile march in from the Ledo Road on February 5, 1944. Fergusson had completed his crossing of the Chindwin by March 5. On March 16 two of his columns captured Lonkin for the benefit of General Stilwell and to encourage him to thrust forward, for it was no use cutting his enemy's communications unless his forces were applying pressure from outside.

But by this time two events had taken place. The Chindit airborne operation had been launched on the night of March 5-6 but Mutaguchi's three divisions had also crossed the Chindwin and were threatening IV Corps' communications.

Calvert's 77th Brigade had been given the task of cutting all communications to the Japanese 18th Division leading north from Indaw. For this task he was given one extra Gurkha battalion, bringing his strength up to six battalions. He planned to place a block on the road and railway in the vicinity of Mawlu with three battalions, leaving two battalions to protect his air base and one battalion to attack the Bhamo-Myitkyina road the other side of the Irrawaddy, where they would co-operate with Colonel Herring's "Dah" Force and the Kachins in that area. Calvert had detailed Major David Monteith to operate along the Irrawaddy to prevent supplies taking that route.

Originally Calvert planned that his brigade would land by glider on two open spaces in the jungle which he had named "Broadway" and "Piccadilly". However, just beforehand, on the evening of March 5, it was found that "Piccadilly" was blocked by teak logs which elephants belonging to the Burma Forest Agency had dragged out to dry prior to their being floated down the Irrawaddy river.

Calvert decided to land all his brigade at "Broadway" and be content with a slower build-up. The descriptions of that fly-in have appeared in several publications, so only a brief account will be given here. The fly-in started on the night of March 5-6. This change of plan at the last moment, and consequent reloading and re-directing of aircraft caused some confusion. As a result, many of the double-tow gliders were released too soon and went astray, and only about two-thirds of the first wave landed accurately. Log paths had indented the landing ground, causing further casualties to gliders on landing, but Calvert finally found that he had enough engineers (mainly American) to complete the airstrip for the landing of transport aircraft. Colonel Alison, (Cochran's second-in-command) took control of the airfield and that night 60 Dakotas landed with their loads. This continued for four nights until 12,000 men and 3,000 mules, a troop of 25-pounders, and a troop of light anti-aircraft artillery had landed, complete with a reserve of stores, food, ammunition, and equipment.

Just south of the Irrawaddy, Brigadier Lentaigne (111th Brigade) landed on the night of March 6-7 in another clearing (Chowringee) and also constructed an airstrip. Chowringee was found to be vulnerable to both air and ground attack and was given up, so the remainder of 111th Brigade landed at "Broadway". During that time there had been no air or ground opposition and both landings were unmolested.

Leaving the 3/9th Gurkhas to garrison "Broadway" with the two King's columns as "floaters", Calvert moved his main force of three battalions straight to the railway to block it. After a short, sharp engagement in which Lieutenant Cairns of the South Staffords won the Victoria Cross, the block christened "White City" (because it later became festooned with supply parachutes) was installed across the railway on March 16 at Henu, about one mile north of Mawlu. The garrison of "White City" immediately got down to the task which it had rehearsed in detail whilst in India, of constructing bombproof dug-outs with the aid of sleepers, ballast, and railway lines from the railway, digging in their telephone lines, sighting their heavy weapons, and erecting a very large amount of barbed wire around platoon, company, and battalion positions, with a belt of wire of World War I dimensions round the entire garrison.

Lentaigne, meanwhile, had managed to get only his brigade headquarters and one column of the 3/4th Gurkhas (30th Column) over the Irrawaddy before they were interrupted. It was decided therefore that the other column of 3/4th Gurkhas (40th Column – Lieutenant-Colonel Morris) would come under the command of Calvert and operate on the Bhamos-Myitkyina road. *En route* to its destination this column blew bridges on the Bhamo-Si-u road and the Bhamo–Namkham road.

This force later became known as "Morris" Force and acted independently of 77th Brigade. Morris formed a safe base in the Kachin hills, from where (with their backs to the Chinese frontiers and protected by Colonel Herring's Kachin levies) his three columns (the 40th, 49th, and 94th) operated against the Bhamo–Myitkyina Road for the next three months until Myitkyina was captured. During this period few, if any, stores in trucks reached Myitkyina by this route. It was unfortunate, however, that Calvert had placed an insufficient block on the Irrawaddy so that stores reached the 18th Division by this water route.

The Cameronians and the King's Own battalions of the 111th Brigade had landed at "Broadway" and were sent post-haste to join their commander, Lentaigne, south of Indaw, where his job was to cut the communications from the south to prevent reinforcements reaching Indaw before Fergusson's 16th Brigade attacked it. These two battalions arrived too late and by March 21 the 24th Independent Mixed Brigade (Hyashi) with three battalions (II/29th, II/51st, and 141st) and elements of the 4th Infantry Regiment had already taken up positions around Indaw. Within a few more days, and after repulsing Fergusson's brigade attack, Hyashi had assembled at Indaw nine battalions, the 138th, 139th, 140th, 141st (24th I.M.B.), I/4th, II/4th, II/29th (4th Infantry Regiment), and III/114th and II/146th Battalions from the 18th and 56th Divisions respectively, complete with artillery and engineers.

Fergusson had marched down from Lonkin quickly, keeping west of the railway. At one period he was deflected towards "White City" when Calvert appeared to be in difficulties from a determined attack by the III/114th Battalion sent down from the 18th Division. This attack was eventually repulsed with heavy losses.

Wingate did not allow Fergusson's brigade time to rest, recuperate, and reconnoitre after its 360-mile march, as he knew that there was a race for the possession of Indaw, Lentaigne having failed to block the route south. Lentaigne had been given a most difficult task because after landing east of the Irrawaddy he was confronted by the problem of crossing the 1,000-yard wide river with his whole brigade and then trying to form a block south of Indaw. This was impracticable and Lentaigne had done well to cross this huge obstacle with his brigade headquarters and one column.

▽ Sappers prepare a bridge for demolition at Henu, "White City". This was to fulfil part of the mission of the Chindits at "White City", which was to cut the road and railway link between Naba and Mogaung. In addition they were to cut the river links between Katha and Myitkyina and the road between Bhamo and Myitkyina.

Fergusson had left the 51st/69th Regiment, R.A., to protect his newly formed airbase at "Aberdeen", about 20 miles due east of "White City", and directed his other three battalions (Leicesters, Queen's, and 45th Reconnaissance Regiment) against Indaw. One of the Queen's columns attacked from the south but the other, moving in from the west, was ambushed and had to withdraw. The Reconnaissance Regiment also hit serious opposition in a waterless zone and also withdrew. But the 2nd Leicesters (Wilkinson), on the other hand, advanced methodically from the north along a range of hills with their flank on the Indawgyi lake. When they met opposition, they dug in and maintained their position for three days against mounting odds before being ordered to break off the engagement.

By this time the Cameronians and King's Own had joined Lentaigne, and the 111th Brigade had at last blown bridges on the railway south of Indaw. There were some major dividends from Fergusson's attack on Indaw besides the casualties the Leicesters in particular had caused. A patrol with an R.A.F. officer in it fortunately found concealed in dry jungle the huge dump of stores which was Mutaguchi's five-day supply reserve for his attack on Imphal and Kohima. Fergusson had the R.A.F. officer in question flown to Assam. From there he directed R.A.F. raids on to the dump until it was destroyed.

The Japanese were now beginning to realise the seriousness of this attack on their communications. When the airborne landings had first been reported on

△ A light plane lands at "White City". The soldiers in the foreground are wearing the felt bush hats which the Japanese took to be Australian.

▽ The end of the railway bridge at Henu. Track and railway ties were used to reinforce the bunker roofs at "White City".

March 9, the cancellation of Mutaguchi's attack on Imphal was considered. But Mutaguchi persuaded Kawabe not to cancel his attack as he was at that time in full flow crossing the Chindwin.

Later he complained when one battalion was sent to join the 24th Independent Mixed Brigade to attack "White City", and when he found that the 5th Air Division was being employed to repulse the invaders rather than assist his own invasion.

The II/146th Battalion from the 56th Division has been despatched to destroy the "Broadway" base, where the main landing had occurred, but Wingate's defence philosophy on the protection of an airbase proved itself. The Japanese were located early by a Burma Rifle reconnaissance patrol who attacked them at a river crossing and inflicted casualties.

Colonel Rome, second-in-command of the 77th Brigade, was in command of "Broadway" with the 3/9th Gurkhas as garrison in a wired-in defensive position along a promontory of trees projecting out into the clearing which was the airfield. Rome's troop of 25-pounders had a field of fire across the flat open ground. He was in touch with the King's (Liver-

2897

pool) floater column nearby. The Japanese crept around onto the perimeter wire and co-ordinated their attack with a bombardment from their two infantry guns from across the airfield. These guns were silenced within minutes by the 25-pounder troop. The Japanese penetrated the perimeter but were quickly ejected by a counter-attack. By this time the King's column was threatening the Japanese rear. After further attacks and counter-attacks during the next few days and a final enveloping movement by the King's which cut off the Japanese and dispersed them, the II/146th Battalion, out of ammunition and supplies and having suffered 150 killed, withdrew carrying their wounded. "Broadway" was never attacked from the ground again.

Earlier on, however, a flight of six R.A.F. Spitfires of No. 81 Squadron was flown in to operate from "Broadway". On March 13 "Broadway" was attacked by 20 "Oscars" (Nakajima Ki-43 *Hayabusa*). Warned by radar installed in the block, five of the Spitfires joined action. The sixth had become damaged on landing and was used to direct the operations of the five aircraft in the air. On this occasion at least four Oscars were shot down

▽ *A Dakota unloads its supplies over a jungle dropping zone. The Chindit columns were almost entirely "teeth" units with their administrative "tail" in India. A radio link to the brigade headquarters, with a simple number code for the stores, meant that re-supply was quick and efficient.*

by the Spitfires and one by the light anti-aircraft Bofors gunners. One of the Spitfires was also shot down.

The 5th Air Division attacked again on March 18. There had been many false alarms meanwhile. Therefore only two Spitfires took off this time. One Japanese formation of about nine aircraft engaged the two Spitfires whilst the remaining 18 Oscars destroyed the three on the ground and attacked other installations. Two Oscars were shot down. Surprisingly little damage had occurred on the ground but the headquarters of the 3rd Tactical Air Force decided to withdraw the remaining two Spitfires instead of reinforcing them and sending in improved radar communications. At that time the R.A.F. had difficulty in seeking out and finding the Japanese Air Force and it might have been more opportune to augment this honeypot in the middle of the jungle to attract the Japanese air forces to an area where they could at least be engaged.

A few days later the 5th Air Division attacked once again with 12 "Sally" (Mitsubishi Ki-21) medium bombers and 20 Oscar fighters. The British light anti-aircraft guns claimed at least six destroyed. Casualties amongst troops well

▷ *Dispatchers push out a load during a drop on Easter Sunday.*
▽ *Two views from circling supply aircraft. The dropping zone or landing ground has been marked out with strips of parachute material. The cords and cloth from parachutes were invaluable for sweat rags and as a tough, light-weight binding.*

dug-in were nil, but a number of light planes were damaged. Craters on the airfield were soon filled in by a maintenance team of bulldozers.

Including one battalion from Mutaguchi's 33rd Division, the Japanese had concentrated 11 battalions with artillery to counter the airborne operation. Practically every Chindit battalion flown in had taken part in a battle and had been "blooded". The Japanese Army Air Force had concentrated on this threat and had neglected the support of the "*U-GO*" offensive across the Chindwin. However, Mutaguchi's threat to Imphal and Kohima was developing. The only reserves trained and equipped to operate in the jungle were the remaining Chindit brigades (the 14th, 23rd, and 3rd West African). These were the brigades which Wingate wanted to keep in hand to relieve the three (the 16th, 77th, and 111th) fighting around Indaw. General Slim, commanding the 14th Army, had to decide whether to use these brigades trained by Wingate for the defence of Imphal and Kohima, or to maintain not only Wingate's offensive but the orders laid down by the Allied high command. Finally he decided that the 14th and 3rd West African Brigades would be flown in to central Burma but that the 23rd Brigade would operate with XXXIII Corps, as a kind of cavalry on its left flank as it advanced south from the Brahmaputra valley to relieve Kohima and Imphal.

By this time on the railway Calvert had decided that he needed more elbow room and had taken the offensive. He attacked and captured Mawlu, which was not well defended, without difficulty. In Mawlu he found a vast amount of documents, which was an unexpected asset for this invasion. Wingate, meanwhile, had visited all brigades at least twice, and then flew to "Aberdeen" to welcome the first elements of the 14th Brigade (Brodie) and the 3rd West African Brigade (Gillmore) which were in process of landing. From his point of view everything was going well. All enemy attacks had been repulsed and he had this force available in the centre of Burma. Lord Mountbatten offered to promote him to Lieutenant-General as he commanded the equivalent of a corps with over 20,000 troops in the field, so that he might speak with more authority to his contemporaries, but Wingate modestly felt that he had not yet proved his hypothesis and so asked Mountbatten to defer the promotion to a later date when his

The American North American B-25J Mitchell attack aircraft

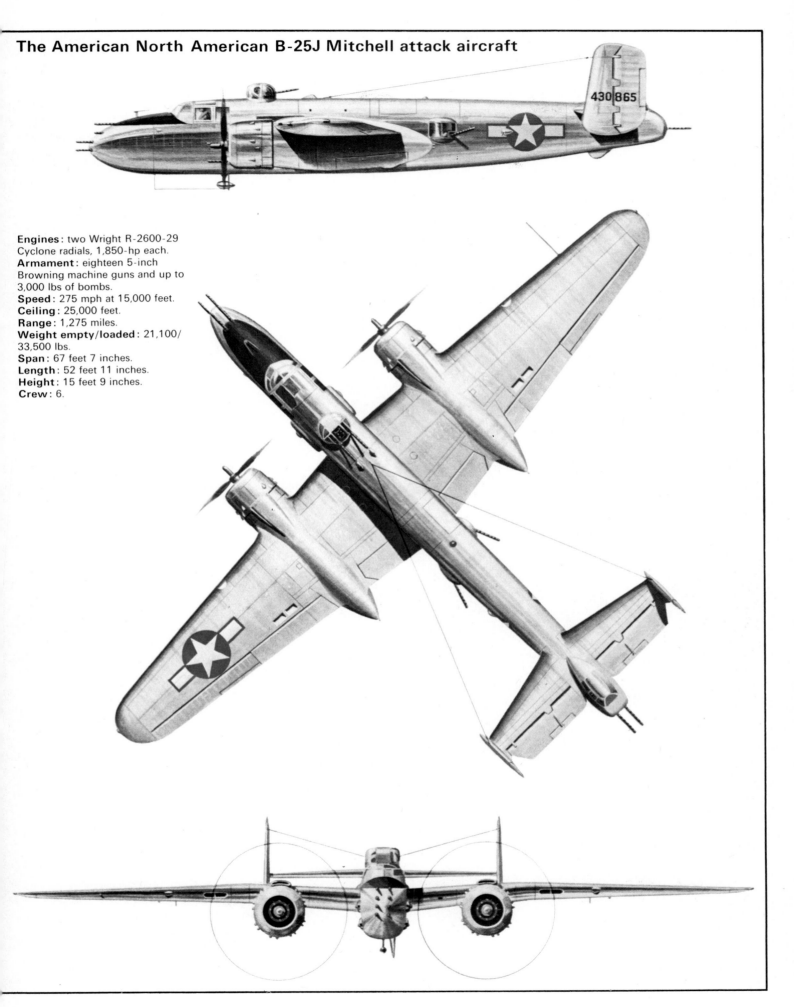

Engines: two Wright R-2600-29
Cyclone radials, 1,850-hp each.
Armament: eighteen 5-inch
Browning machine guns and up to
3,000 lbs of bombs.
Speed: 275 mph at 15,000 feet.
Ceiling: 25,000 feet.
Range: 1,275 miles.
Weight empty/loaded: 21,100/
33,500 lbs.
Span: 67 feet 7 inches.
Length: 52 feet 11 inches.
Height: 15 feet 9 inches.
Crew: 6.

△ ◁ ◁ *Mawlu after its capture.*
△ ◁ *Colonel Gatey, Major Gaitley, Wingate, and Lieutenant-Colonel Walter Scott at "Broadway".*
△ △ *A captured Japanese gun.*
△ *Japanese trucks caught in an ambush by the 7th Nigeria Rgt.*
◁ *A signaller with an antenna slung between the trees. Besides calling for supplies, the radio link enabled the Chindits to give targets for the fighters and bombers of the Air Commando.*

methods of operations had been proved by victory and a withdrawal of the Japanese.

But it was not to be in his lifetime. Returning from "Broadway" in an American Mitchell bomber he touched down at Imphal for a conference with Air-Marshal Sir John Baldwin, commander of the 3rd Tactical Air Force. After the conference they both took off, Wingate's plane leading. The last Baldwin saw of him was in the red evening light. Six minutes later the Mitchell bomber had unaccountably dived at cruising speed into the forward slopes of the Silchar plain, where lay his destination. All aboard were killed. Some form of sabotage seems the only credible explanation.

On March 12 General Kawabe, G.O.C.-in-C. Burma Area Army, had ordered Major-General Hyashi, commanding the 24th Independent Mixed Brigade, to clear the length of the railway line of airborne troops. The 56th Division had also detailed II/146th Battalion which attacked "Broadway" and was defeated. The III/114th Battalion came from the 18th Division and had already attacked "White City" and had been severely repulsed. The II/51st from the 15th Division arrived in time to take part in some of the fighting, but was then sent back to rejoin its own division as it advanced over the Chindwin. Hyashi had therefore the equivalent of a division in strength. He had previously driven off Fergusson's 16th Brigade in its attempt to capture Indaw airfield. He now decided to attack and remove the "White City" block. On the night of April 5-6, after a heavy bombardment, Hyashi launched his attack. The defenders of "White City" had a clear field of fire over paddy fields to the west and south, so Hyashi concentrated mainly on the jungle-covered east and northern perimeters. He attacked initially with three battalions. They were held up on the wire, where they received heavy casualties from a rain of up to 1,000 mortar shells and the fire of Vickers machine guns trained along the wire. He attacked again before dawn but with no further advance. He lodged a company in the hills on the north side of the block but in the morning Mustang fighter-bombers, diving again and again, bombed, strafed, and destroyed this force. Hyashi withdrew out of range and decided on his next move. In the meantime he was bombed repeatedly by both Mustangs and Mitchell medium bombers belonging to No. 1 Air

Commando and directed from an observation post in "White City" which overlooked the plain. The following night Hyashi attacked again with fresh troops. These were armed with Bangalore torpedoes to burst their way through the wire, but all the torpedo teams were destroyed. A further attack later on in the night met with the same result. During the nights Dakotas replenished the block's ammunition and rations. The block itself was only 1,000 yards long by the railway and only 800 yards deep, but it consisted of a number of small hills up to 100 feet high, which made a series of defiles within the block.

This time Hyashi deployed two tanks in front of Mawlu, which was his base, but both tanks were hit by anti-tank 2-pounders from "White City". Hyashi attacked for the next three nights with fresh troops, bringing all seven battalions into the attack, but to no avail. The rain of 2-inch and 3-inch mortar bombs, grenades, and deadly Vickers machine gun fire would not allow his men to penetrate the block. Some 700,000 rounds of belted medium machine gun ammunition were delivered by air to the block during the period. During the day Hyashi's forming up and administrative areas were severely bombed two or three times by Mustangs, Mitchell bombers and, on occasion, British Vultee Vengeance dive-bombers. Hyashi had one trump card: a 6-inch mortar, which only had a short range of 1,500 yards but whose large missile could penetrate some of the "White City" dug-outs, which were heavily camouflaged. Some bombing by the 5th Air Division had achieved no other results than the fact that about eight of the medium bombers were shot down by the six Bofors anti-aircraft guns which had been introduced into the block the night before the attack began. The troop of 25-pounders in the block faced Mawlu and carried out counter-battery fire which reduced the effectiveness of Hyashi's own artillery.

On April 10, Major-General Lentaigne, who was Wingate's successor, flew into "White City". He gave orders that Calvert should form a counter-attack force to attack the Japanese base from outside the block. Brigadier Gillmore became commander of the "White City" block, still under Calvert's command. Inside the block the garrison would continue to be the 1st South Staffords, the 6th Nigeria Regiment, and one column and all the

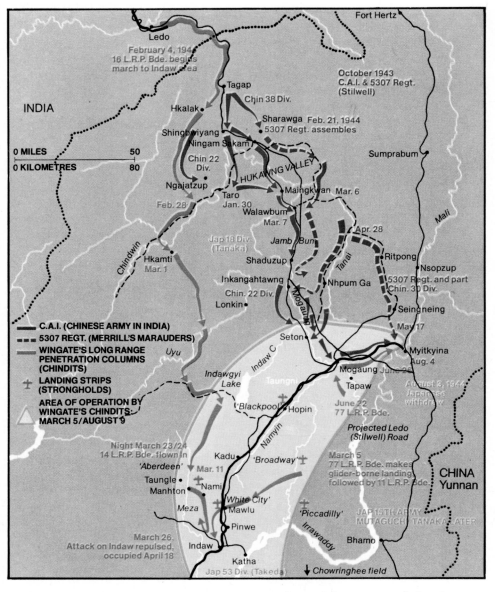

The map contains the following labels:

Fort Hertz

Ledo
February 4, 1944
16 L.R.P. Bde. begins
march to Indaw area

INDIA

October 1943
C.A.I. & 5307 Regt.
(Stilwell)

Tagap
Chin 38 Div.

Hkalak

Sharawga Feb. 21, 1944
Shingbwiyang 5307 Regt. assembles
Ningam Sakam

Sumprabum

0 MILES 50
0 KILOMETRES 80

Chin 22
Div.

Mali

Ngajatzup

Taro
Jan. 30

Maingkwan Mar. 6

HUKAWNG VALLEY

Walawbum
Feb. 28 Mar. 7

Apr. 28

Chindwin

Hkamti
Mar. 1

Jap 18 Div.
(Tanaka)

Jamb Bum

Ritpong

Nsopzup

Shaduzup

Tanai

Inkangahtawng

Nhpum Ga

5307 Regt. and part
Chin. 30 Div.

Chin. 22 Div.

Lonkin

Seingneing

Mogaung

May 17

Seton

Myitkyina
Aug. 4

Uyu

Indaw C

Mogaung June 26

Indawgyi
Lake

Taungni

Tapaw

August 3, 1944
Japanese
withdraw

'Blackpool' Hopin

June 22
77 L.R.P. Bde.

Namyin

Projected Ledo
(Stilwell) Road

C.A.I. (CHINESE ARMY IN INDIA)
5307 REGT. (MERRILL'S MARAUDERS)
WINGATE'S LONG RANGE
PENETRATION COLUMNS
(CHINDITS)
LANDING STRIPS
(STRONGHOLDS)
AREA OF OPERATION BY
WINGATE'S CHINDITS
MARCH 5/AUGUST 9

Night March 23/24
14 L.R.P. Bde. flown in

Kadu 'Broadway'

March 5
77 L.R.P. Bde. makes
glider-borne landing
followed by 11 L.R.P. Bde.

CHINA
Yunnan

'Aberdeen'

Taungle
Manhton Nami

'White City'

'Piccadilly'

JAP 15TH ARMY
MUTAGUCHI TANAKA LATER

Meza Mawlu

Irrawaddy

Bhamo

March 26,
Attack on Indaw repulsed,
occupied April 18

Pinwe

Indaw

Katha
Jap 53 Div. (Takeda)

↓ Chowringhee field

△ *The second Chindit operation, with the U.S., Chinese, and British drive from the north that was the reason for the Chindits' continued activities.*

mortars and machine guns of the Lancashire Fusiliers. Calvert formed his new force, about 2,600 strong and consisting of the 3/6th Gurkhas, 1st Reconnaissance Regiment (from the 16th Brigade), and the 7th Nigerians, plus one column of Lancashire Fusiliers. At about 0400 hours on April 8 Calvert attacked Mawlu and Sepein. Hyashi put in his two reserve battalions, but not before Calvert had captured Mawlu station and Sepein, and overrun a number of his headquarters, including the artillery one. However, the British forces were spread out too widely and lost momentum. They withdrew after dark. Hyashi continued his offensive against "White City" that night. The next day Hyashi heard reports that his communications with Indaw had been cut by a Nigerian regiment. The following day his rear area was attacked in strength by the 3/6th Gurkhas and the Reconnaissance Regiment. His administrative areas and headquarters were overrun and severe

fighting broke out in the jungle south-east of Mawlu. This carried on throughout the day in spite of improvised counter-attacks. Hyashi was uncertain of the strength of these attacks and continued his attack against "White City". The following day his administrative areas and gun positions were further penetrated from the south and he found himself jammed between the barbed wire of "White City" and the counter-attacking force in his rear. He led one last desperate charge in which he himself was killed. His forces were counter-attacked by the 6th Nigerians from "White City" and attacked again and again by the Gurkhas and the Reconnaissance Regiment. The finale occurred just after 1300 hours when the remains of the Independent Mixed Brigade and the 4th Infantry Regiment were preparing a *banzai* counter-attack. At this moment 27 Mustangs were directed on to them when they were in close order in flat jungle. Very great casualties resulted, which caused the Japanese to start a withdrawal, but the 77th Brigade did not follow up. All that evening the forces of the 24th Independent Mixed Brigade withdrew towards their base at Indaw, being harassed *en route* by small units of the Lancashire Fusiliers and the 7th Leicestershire Regiment. The previous night the lorry park at Tonlong had been severely attacked by the Leicesters and over 80 trucks had been destroyed. By April 17 the remains of the 24th Independent Mixed Brigade had withdrawn to Indaw.

So, to sum up, this force of divisional strength had by April 18 been severely defeated by British forces consisting of four British battalions, one Gurkha battalion, and two Nigerian battalions, well supported from the air.

Whilst this fighting was taking place around "White City", the 111th Brigade had destroyed enemy supply dumps near Banmauk and 14th Brigade had destroyed the main railway bridge over the Bonchaung Gorge as well as several other bridges on the way to Indaw. Lentaigne had ordered a further attack on Indaw. The 16th Brigade advanced and overran Indaw West airfield, destroying installations and other *matériel*. Between April 22 and 27, the 14th Brigade destroyed 21 dumps of supplies and ammunition, and 15,000 gallons of petrol, and cut the railway south of the town in 16 places, whilst leaving mines and booby traps throughout the area. This effectively destroyed he lines of communication to the Japanese 31st Division attacking Kohima and the 15th Division attacking Imphal. One Japanese transport column of 150 vehicles was left stranded between Banmauk and Homalin and took no further part in supplying the 33rd Division.

East of the Irrawaddy, "Morris" Force had achieved a series of successes against the Bhamo–Myitkyina road, including destroying the main road over the Taping river at Myothit and capturing and destroying Nalong. These Gurkhas were tireless over the next few weeks, in spite of a shortage of explosives and supplies, in attacking and repeatedly destroying bridges and convoys on this road.

It might be said that by the end of April the Chindit forces were raging rampant across all the Japanese communications in north Burma, weakening to the point of destruction the Japanese divisions operating against the 14th Army and General Stilwell's forces. It was at this time, after Wingate's death, that it was decided to make a drastic change of plan. Here we will not discuss all the political ramifications which brought about this change, but just record the events.

A change of plan

South-East Asia Command had decided that the Chindit forces should cease to operate against the lines of communication leading to Mutaguchi's forces attacking Imphal and Kohima, and concentrate on assisting Stilwell's forces in capturing the objectives laid down in the "Quadrant" and "Sextant" Conferences, i.e. Mogaung and Myitkyina and an area south of it. To achieve this result it was decided that with the approach of the monsoon, "Aberdeen", "White City", and "Broadway" would be given up and a block placed on the railway and road nearer Stilwell's forces by a reconstituted 111th Brigade under Major (later Brigadier) Masters, General Lentaigne's original brigade major. The 77th Brigade, consisting of the South Staffords, the Lancashire Fusiliers, and the 3/6th Gurkhas, should move north to protect this block from the east. The 14th Brigade should take over "White City" and carry out its evacuation, and the 3rd West African Brigade should move north to protect this new block, which was to be named "Blackpool", from the west. The 16th Brigade would be flown out. The 111th Brigade would consist of its two original British battalions and the 30th Column Gurkha Rifles, but in addition would be reinforced by the 3/9th Gurkhas, and the King's (Liverpool) Regiment from the 77th Brigade.

This plan did not work. Masters had not seen "White City", nor had his force been trained to install a defensive block with barbed wire, artillery, airfields, and anti-aircraft defences. The area chosen did not cover the railway line or road, but instead was placed on a jungle-covered spur jutting out into the valley, open to artillery bombardment. Soon after it was installed with inadequate wire, the block was overrun with severe casualties. The 77th Brigade, from the opposite side of the flooded valley, was unable to assist, whilst the West African Brigade had been diverted to Lake Indawgyi to protect the area whilst Catalina flying boats flew out many sick and wounded. The 14th Brigade, which had taken over the "White City" block and cleverly evacuated it before the forward elements of the 53rd Division attacked it, marched north and operated meanwhile in different areas in the hills west of the railway. In fact, apart from a brisk action at Kyusunlai Pass, the 14th Brigade and the West African Brigade eventually got stuck down in the malarial areas of Lake Indawgyi. There, seeing their comrades being flown out, many succumbed to temptation and a large exodus of sick occurred, greater than was warrantable under the rules for evacuation laid down by Wingate. As a result, for nearly six weeks these two brigades took practically no offensive action. This was partly the result of the marching and counter-marching caused by Lentaigne's and Slim's change of plan.

At the fall of "Blackpool", Stilwell, who was advancing towards Kamaing, was naturally very annoyed as the way was now open for reinforcements from the south to reach Mogaung and Myitkyina. By a *coup-de-main*, Merrill's Marauders and a Chinese regiment had seized Myitkyina airfield on May 17. This *coup-de-main* changed the whole face of the war in north Burma. Calvert's 77th Brigade was ordered forward to attack Mogaung, whilst Stilwell flew in 30,000 reinforcements to Myitkyina airfield to capture the town. Meanwhile "Morris" Force, on the east bank of the Irrawaddy, was asked to do all it could to attack all the Japanese garrisons on the eastern bank opposite the town of Myitkyina.

△ *Major-General W. D. A. "Joe" Lentaigne, who began the expedition commanding the 111th Brigade, but on Wingate's death took overall command of the Special Force. Though an excellent leader, he did not have the unorthodox genius of the original creator and leader of the Chindits.*

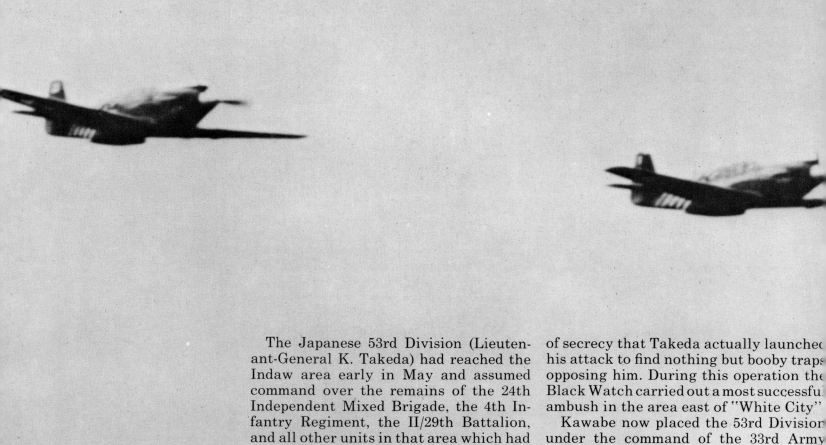

The Japanese 53rd Division (Lieutenant-General K. Takeda) had reached the Indaw area early in May and assumed command over the remains of the 24th Independent Mixed Brigade, the 4th Infantry Regiment, the II/29th Battalion, and all other units in that area which had been defeated by the Chindits. Takeda was ordered to launch a further attack on "White City". He brought up two regiments supported by a strong force of artillery, but (as related) the 14th Brigade (Brodie) side-stepped with such a degree of secrecy that Takeda actually launched his attack to find nothing but booby traps opposing him. During this operation the Black Watch carried out a most successful ambush in the area east of "White City".

Kawabe now placed the 53rd Division under the command of the 33rd Army (Lieutenant-General Honda), which had assumed command of 18th and 56th Division in the Hukawng valley and Salween fronts respectively. He left the remains of the 24th Independent Mixed Brigade to hold the Indaw area under the direct con-

△ P-51 Mustangs roar over the strip at "Broadway". Like the Mitchell beneath them, they are marked with the five-stripes insignia of the Air Commando.
◁ A B-25 attacks a Japanese store and supply depot.
▷ Cochran with Captain John Birkett and a British officer.

trol of the 33rd Army. Takeda, on finding "White City" evacuated, moved quickly up the railway line in time to prevent the installation of the 111th Brigade's "Black-pool" block. In the destruction of "Black-pool" the 53rd Division suffered some 500 casualties.

At this time the 18th Division (Tanaka) was holding Kamaing against Stilwell's forces, but a Chinese regiment cut its communications and after a long battle the 18th Division was forced to withdraw. The 12 Chinese divisions on the Salween were still quiescent, so that when the Marauders struck Myitkyina, the 56th Division was able to send General Mizu-kami with a battalion and other units to hold Myitkyina at all costs. Mizukami, with about 3,000 men, held out in Myit-kyina for 76 days although outnumbered by about 15 to 1.

Honda (33rd Army) had planned to use the 53rd Division (Takeda) to relieve the 18th Division (Tanaka) but Tanaka asked to stay where he was. Honda therefore despatched the 53rd Division to retake

Myitkyina. But just at that time at the beginning of June, the 77th Brigade (Calvert) started its attack on Mogaung, the base for which had been brilliantly seized by Calvert's second-in-command, Colonel Rome. The distance between his base in the hills and Mogaung town proper, with the big railway bridge over the Mogaung river, was only about 5,000 yards. But this whole area consists mainly of mangrove swamps and flooded paddy fields before the elevated ground around the town proper is reached. Calvert protected his rear by seizing Tapaw and asked an American O.S.S. agent, Lieutenant Davis, to organise a screen of scouts on his flanks. He then started his attack with 2,000 men and no artillery, monsoon conditions precluding the construction of an airfield. He had orders to take Mogaung at all costs. Initially things went well and a large hospital and ordnance area were overrun, yielding some 50 prisoners. Calvert was then faced with the crossing of the sluggish, deep stream called the Wetthauk Chaung. A direct attack on the bridge at Pinhmi failed with heavy casualties, but fortunately the 3/6th Gurkhas found a ford and Calvert struck at night across this ford and cut the road behind the Pinhmi garrison. The Gurkhas were then launched into the attack from the rear and soon overcame the defences of the bridge.

However, it will be remembered that the 53rd Division had been ordered to recapture Myitkyina. But the appearance of the 77th Brigade so close to Mogaung

caused General Honda once again to review his plan. He immediately ordered the headquarters of the 128th Regiment into Mogaung and told Takeda to abandon the contemplated attack on Myitkyina and to concentrate his division for the defence of Mogaung.

Calvert's depleted forces were now encountering very heavy artillery concentrations, which they had some difficulty in avoiding by digging into that flooded area. However, he was close to American air force bases and air support was excellent. From observation on the 1,100-foot Umantaung Hill his R.A.F. adviser, Squadron-Leader Thompson, and his men could observe the artillery fire emanating from in and around Mogaung and direct the U.S.A.A.F. Mustangs down onto their targets. Where the distance was within mortar range these targets would be indicated by mortar smoke. Calvert quickly obtained some 4.2-inch and 81-mm mortars which, from Pinhmi, could bombard Mogaung and bring down harassing fire all night. This air superiority was so effective that the Japanese were chary of firing during the day-time. On one occasion a battalion of the 53rd Division was advancing out of the town for its first action since leaving Formosa when Squadron-Leader Thompson was able to bring down 27 Mustangs on to it and catch the troops in the open, destroying most of them. Mogaung, between the Mogaung river and the flooded Namyin Chaung, became a bomb trap for the Japanese 53rd Division.

In the meantime, Stilwell's Chinese had not been idle and, with a second right hook behind the redoubtable 18th Division, succeeded in destroying most of the 18th Division's artillery. In fact the 18th Division had been reduced to a strength of about 3,000 all ranks and was told to take to the hills and concentrate in the area of Sahmaw. This was between June 7 and 22.

The 77th Brigade's attack on Mogaung developed further until the 3/6th Gurkhas and the South Staffords faced Mogaung across 200 yards of paddy, with the remains of the Lancashire Fusiliers and a

△ *A Japanese bunker at Mogaung. The town became a death trap for the Japanese, who came under accurate and deadly attacks by the Mustangs of the Air Commando directed onto their targets by the Chindit forward air controllers.*

portion of the King's Regiment in reserve. As a result of casualties and sickness, Calvert's attacking strength was now under 1,000. At this time Calvert sent a patrol to make contact with the Chinese forces moving south from Kamaing. The Chinese 114th Regiment was contacted and with the aid of 77th Brigade's ranger boats it crossed the river on June 17 and took up positions on Calvert's left. The addition of its 25-pounder battery was very welcome to the British brigade. Calvert agreed with Colonel Li to attack the following day. After good air support the previous night, the 77th Brigade laid down a barrage of 1,500 rounds of mortar ammunition at 0230 hours, and the attack started. The Gurkhas and South Staffords achieved their objective but the Chinese had not advanced. It took a hard counter-

attack by the Lancashire Fusiliers and a Bladet detachment of flame-throwers to destroy the redoubt which had been the cause of most of the casualties that day. The following day, and the next, Calvert used all his reserves, including his brigade headquarters and animal transport company, to maintain the offensive until Mogaung was taken on June 26. The Chinese 2/114th Battalion had occupied Loilaw and, in the latter stages, had co-operated with Calvert's attack, suffering three casualties.

The 77th Brigade had suffered about 1,500 casualties in its attack on Mogaung, and a commission of British and American doctors calculated that there were only 300 fit men left in the brigade.

General Lentaigne had urged the 111th Brigade to attack west of the railway. In that area all three brigades (111th, 14th, and 3rd West African) had suffered severely from cerebral malaria and tick typhus, which had lowered morale. Masters re-formed his brigade into one large company and attacked Japanese positions on the tops of hills in the Padiga area, and then held these against counter-attack. During one attack Major Blaker, M.C., of the Highland Light Infantry, attached to the 3/9th Gurkhas, gained a posthumous Victoria Cross. This was the fourth Victoria Cross won by the Chindits. Two more were gained by Lieutenant Michael Almand and Rifleman Tulbahadur Pun, both of the 3/6th Gurkha Rifles, during the final assault on Mogaung.

Stilwell was still pressing his forces forward. Myitkyina had not yet been taken. After ordering a medical investigation, Lord Louis Mountbatten gave direct orders to Stilwell to evacuate the 77th and 111th Brigades at once, accusing him of keeping these two brigades in action for far too long. The 14th and the 3rd West African Brigades were directed on to the railway town of Taugni south of Mogaung, which they occupied on August 12. The 3rd West African Brigade had taken over Sahmaw on August 9.

All brigades were flown out, but the mules were left behind as transport for the 36th British Division (Festing) to take over. However, this division improvised jeep transport on the railway line which it used in its advance south to Indaw.

On August 1, Mizukami, in command of the Myitkyina garrison, ordered Colonel Maruyama to withdraw the remnants of his regiment from Myitkyina. Mizukami himself then committed suicide. Stilwell had now achieved all his objectives. Myitkyina and Mogaung were captured and both the road and a safe air route to China were now open. An oil pipeline was soon pushed through to Kunming. Stilwell continued to advance with his forces in a three-pronged offensive south from Myitkyina and Mogaung. The 36th Division was directed to secure the Indaw-Katha area, the Chindits' old hunting ground. The Chinese 22nd Division crossed the Irrawaddy near "Broadway" and the Chinese 38th Division was directed on to Bhamo. The Japanese 53rd Division and remnants of the 18th Division had not much fight left in them and withdrew, leaving only small rearguards to slow down their enemy. The Chinese "Yoke" Force on the Salween had at last taken action and linked up with Stilwell's forces at Bhamo. By December 1 the 36th Division, having swept through the old Chindit areas, had captured Indaw and Wuntho and had made patrol contact with the 14th Army, which had not yet crossed the Chindwin in force.

Results of the Chindit campaign

The keystone of the arch of the Japanese defence of Burma had fallen. Wingate's operations in the centre of Burma had thus proved the policy of indirect approach. By landing in the centre of the Japanese lines of communication and cutting them, they had let in the American/Chinese forces from the north and east so that they had got behind the Japanese forces facing the 14th Army west of the Chindwin. When this occurred the 33rd Army facing Slim had to swing right back to face north, opening the way at last for Slim's forces, which had been stuck in the hills. After that, Slim had no difficulty in bridging the Chindwin and continuing his slow advance. By this time Rees' 19th Indian Division had linked up with the 36th British Division. Slim had planned a set-piece operation called "Capital" which had been approved by the Chiefs-of-Staff in Washington and London, but Stilwell's rapid advance, once contact with the Chindits had been gained, had put "Capital" out of date. Slim therefore had to reorganise his plans to attack south of Mandalay in an improvised plan which was known as "Extended Capital".

There can be no doubt that the Chindit campaign was successful. Without it, the conquest of north Burma could not have taken place. The Chindits kept Japanese communications to the forces opposing Stilwell blocked for at least three months, and destroyed two of the 33rd Army's three lines of communication whilst it was attacking IV Corps and then the 14th Army. Later, coming up from the south, the Chindits captured one of Stilwell's objectives and "Morris" Force materially helped in the capture of the second objective, Myitkyina. Once these objectives had been taken and the two Japanese

divisions, the 18th and 53rd, as well as the 24th Independent Mixed Brigade, had been largely destroyed, the way was open for Stilwell's forces, including the British 36th Division, to advance down south and turn the Japanese position facing the 14th Army. The Chindits, consisting of about 20 battalions with not more than one battery of field artillery and one battery of anti-aircraft artillery, had with their air support, first of all, defeated the 11 Japanese battalions eventually brought together under the 24th Independent Mixed Brigade. Three of these battalions had been drawn from divisions facing the frontiers of Burma. Secondly, the Burma Area commander's reserve, 53rd Division, instead of being available to help the 33rd Army in its offensive against Imphal, was directed against the airborne forces. This

△ *Gurkha and British troops return from the second expedition behind the Japanese lines. Air transport had now almost ceased to be a novelty for many soldiers, but the man on the left appears to be observing his flight with some apprehension.*

The CHINDITS

45 RECCE REGT
ROYAL REGT OF ARTILLERY
CORPS OF ROYAL ENGINEERS
ROYAL CORPS OF SIGNALS
2ND QUEEN'S ROYAL REGT
1ST KING'S OWN ROYAL REGT
1ST & 13TH KING'S REGT
1ST BEDS & HERTS REGT
2ND LEICESTERSHIRE REGT
7TH LEICESTERSHIRE REGT
1ST LANCASHIRE FUSILIERS
1ST CAMERONIANS
2ND DUKE OF WELLINGTON'S REGT
4TH BORDER REGT
1ST SOUTH STAFFORDSHIRE REGT
2ND BLACK WATCH (RHR)
1ST ESSEX REGT
2ND YORK & LANCASTER REGT
142 COMMANDO

ROYAL ARMY CHAPLAIN'S DEPT
R A S C
R C M P
R I A S C
ROYAL ARMY MEDICAL CORPS
ROYAL ARMY ORDNANCE CORPS
R E M E
3/2 GURKHA RIFLES
3/4 GURKHA RIFLES
3/6 GURKHA RIFLES
3/9 GURKHA RIFLES
4/9 GURKHA RIFLES
2ND BURMA RIFLES
6TH NIGERIAN REGT RWAFF
7TH NIGERIAN REGT RWAFF
12TH NIGERIAN REGT RWAFF
HONG KONG VOLUNTEERS
ROYAL AIR FORCE
No 1 AIR COMMAND USAAF

BURMA 1942-1944

THE BOLDEST MEASURES ARE THE SAFEST

OLD COMRADES ASSOCIATION

△ *The colours of the Old Comrades Association. The actions fought on the two expeditions are displayed on either side of the figure of the Chinthe, or mythical dragon, which guards Burmese temples and from whose name Wingate coined the title Chindits.*

division received 500 casualties at "Blackpool" and very heavy casualties at Mogaung. The Japanese 5th Air Division had also been diverted from operations on the Imphal front to deal with the airborne forces. All this time the numbers of aircraft feeding and supplying the Chindits were never more than one-seventh of the total aircraft supplying the remainder of the forces in Burma, and the quantity of stores dropped also never exceeded one-seventh, in any one month, of the total stores supplied in Burma from the air. So, judging the whole campaign in retrospect, it can be said that the main reason for the defeat of the nine Japanese divisions operating on interior lines in Burma in 1944 was primarily the operations of Wingate's Chindits. The force achieved this by coming in from the third dimension – the air – and forming a fifth front across the Japanese lines of communication.

During the period after Wingate's death, from May to August, the Chindit forces lost 3,786 killed, wounded, and missing. For the period from March to May the numbers, including missing, were just over 1,100, making a total of about 5,000 killed, wounded, and missing. Compared with this, the total casualties in the northern front between January and August 19, 1944 were estimated at 13,000 Chinese and about 1,300 American. But it must never be forgotten that the conquest of Burma from the land could not have been achieved in any way whatsoever without the operations of the R.A.F. and U.S.A.A.F., with the United States 1st Air Commando, under Cochran, always in the van.

CHAPTER 174
Imphal and Kohima

Previous page: *The winding road to Tamu. To the left is the hill known as "Crete West", on the south-west perimeter around the strategically vital town of Imphal, besieged by the Japanese 15th and 33rd Divisions.*

△ *Naga tribesmen at work road clearing in the Imphal-Kohima area.*

△▷ *A British tank patrols the Imphal–Ukhrul road just before the Japanese complete the investment of the Imphal area.*

▽▷ *The Imphal–Kohima road, cut when the Japanese 15th Division reached Kanglatongi on March 29.*

The so-called "March on Delhi", the Japanese offensive against the British IV Corps on the Tiddim-Imphal-Kohima front which started rolling when Lieutenant-General G. Yanagida's 33rd Division crossed the Chindwin in force on the night of March 7-8, was the brainchild of Lieutenant-General Renya Mutaguchi, aged 55.

To the Japanese it was known as the *"U-GO"* offensive and its limited objectives was to forestall a British offensive by attacking and destroying the British base at Imphal, thus strengthening the Japanese defence of Burma.

A subsidiary objective was, with the use of the Indian National Army division raised and commanded by the plausible and resourceful Subhas Chandra Bhose, to "exercise political control over India". This was to be achieved by encouraging and supporting dissident anti-British elements, who had in the previous year created a most serious situation in Bengal and Bihar by their widespread sabotage of bridges, communications, and airfields. As it happened Chandra Bhose stayed comfortably in Rangoon and the I.N.A. division, which had the strength of only a brigade (totalling about 7,000 men), had

little effect on either the battle or the political situation.

The date of the *"U-GO"* offensive was timed to phase in with the successful outcome of Major-General T. Sakurai's *"HA-GO"* offensive in the Arakan. The latter's purpose was to draw off the Allied reserve divisions to the Arakan prior to Mutaguchi's attack on Imphal. This task Sakurai's 55th Division had successfully achieved for, by the end of February 1944, six divisions (5th, 7th, 25th, 26th, 36th, and 81st West African), a parachute brigade, and a special service (commando) brigade, had been drawn into that theatre. This concentration, coupled with the extensive use of air supply, had certainly foiled Sakurai's raid after three weeks of hard fighting. But Mutaguchi should have crossed the Chindwin in mid-February as planned in order to take the maximum advantage of Sakurai's feint.

Unfortunately Lieutenant-General M. Yamauchi's 15th Division, which Mutaguchi intended to use for the direct assault on Imphal, had become stuck in Siam. It was not until February 11, after Mutaguchi himself had signalled Field-Marshal Count Terauchi, command-

er of the Southern Army at Singapore, that the 15th Division started to concentrate in Burma, arriving ill-equipped, ill-fed, and ill-tempered.

This division had been training in northern Siam and some of its units had been improving the Chiengmai–Toungoo road as an alternative route to the much bombed Burma–Siam railway. Assisted by ten motor transport companies, it had marched the 700-mile long road from Chiengmai to Shwebo via Kentung and Mandalay in order to toughen itself up and prepare itself for its task ahead.

D-day for the "U-GO" offensive was fixed for March 15, by which time the 15th Division must not only be re-equipped but have moved to its start line between Paungbyin and Sittaung on the Chindwin, as well as organising its communications forward from Indaw and Wuntho on the railway via Pinlebu.

The other two divisions in Mutaguchi's 15th Army were in a much better state.

The 33rd Division had operated for many years in China and had taken part from the start in the conquest of Burma as well as combatting the first Chindit operation in 1943. This division, advancing initially along comparatively good roads, would carry with it all the armour and heavy artillery (4th Tank Regiment, 1st Anti-Tank Battalion, 3rd and 18th Heavy Field Artillery Regiments) that the Japanese could muster for this attack.

The 31st Division (Lieutenant-General K. Sato), whose task was the unenviable one of advancing from Homalin and Tamanthi on the upper reaches of the Chindwin river, and then over a series of parallel ridges (reaching a height of over 7,000 feet) to Jessami and Kohima, had previously operated only in China, although some of its units had been stationed on islands in the Pacific. It had arrived in Burma between June and September 1943 and had immediately been sent to the Chindwin front, where it had crossed swords with the battle-experienced 20th Indian Division (Major-General D.D. Gracey). The 31st Division had had, therefore, plenty of time to get inured to the conditions in that area. It would operate on a mule and horse transport basis, trusting on a tenuous 100-mile long line of communications from Mawlu and Indaw on the railway to Tamanthi and Homalin, supported by a three-week reserve of food, ammunition, and fodder built up on the line of the Chindwin.

Mutaguchi, "the victor of Singapore", had previously commanded the 18th Division in north Burma and had been most impressed by the activities of the Chindits and their leader, Brigadier Wingate, whom he held in high regard. Mutaguchi had, with some difficulty, sold his plan to knock out IV Corps by a three-pronged, three-divisional thrust against the 200-mile road leading down from the Brahmaputra valley parallel to the Chindwin. Prime Minister Tojo and Count Terauchi agreed to this gamble only because they needed some offensive success to offset the disasters which had been occurring in the Pacific. They then agreed only with the proviso that it should be combined with an attempt to start widespread insurrection in East India with the co-operation of Subhas Chandra Bhose's Indian National Army, on which they placed great hopes of success.

Lieutenant-General M. Kawabe, commanding the Burma Area Army, was sceptical of the whole plan and had

orders to prevent Mutaguchi from over-reaching himself. Lieutenant-General Tazoe, commanding the 5th Air Division, had no faith in Mutaguchi's plan whatso-ever. He was apprehensive of what the Allied airborne forces (the Chindits) would do, a force that his reconnaissance aircraft had shown were ready to be sent in again. He pointed out to Mutaguchi that he would be totally incapable of helping him with air supply once he had crossed the Chindwin.

Mutaguchi's plan was for the 33rd Division, with the bulk of his armour and artillery, to advance from its bridgehead at Kalewa and to attack and surround the 17th Indian Division (Major-General D.T. Cowan) at Tiddim and Tongzang. Leaving a small containing force, the 33rd Division would push forward with all speed north-wards to the Imphal plain, where it would also cut the Bishenpur Track running west to Silchar. One regiment,

under Major-General T. Yamamoto, would meanwhile advance north from Kalemyo up the Kabaw valley and open a road through to support the 15th Division, bringing most of the wheeled and track vehicles with it.

The 33rd Division would start its ad-vance one week before D-day, when the 15th and 31st Divisions would cross the Chindwin.

The 15th Division's task was to cross the Chindwin near Thaungdut and ad-vance on tracks via Ukhrul to cut the Dimapur road north of Imphal near Kanglatongbi. It would also detail one column to contain the 20th Division (Gracey) east of Palel. With the 33rd Division, its final objective was to overrun the rich Imphal plain, destroy IV Corps, and capture the airfields and a vast quantity of supplies.

The 31st Division had the more arduous task of advancing 70 to 100 miles along

△ *A Bren gun team of the R.A.F. Regiment in position above an airfield in the Imphal valley. Airfield defence was of primary importance in the Imphal campaign, for without it the besieged defenders could not have received the supplies needed for their 88-day defence.*

▽ *Ancient and modern in Burma: an ox cart crosses an airfield in front of a "Hurribomber" being prepared for a sortie.*
▽▷ *The town of Kohima, severely mauled by the Japanese siege.*
Page 2920: *Allied troops move up the "Chocolate Staircase" en route to Tiddim Village, south of Imphal.*

footpaths from the riverine villages of Tamanthi and Homalin, through the Naga Hills, and over a series of bare mountain ranges to capture Kohima, a small, obscure village and staging post on a 4,000-foot pass on the Dimapur–Imphal road. Whether it would exploit its success from there by attacking the undefended railhead at Dimapur depended on circumstances.

Mutaguchi hoped that the whole operation would be resolved within three weeks, by which time he also hoped to have road communications functioning from Kalewa via Palel to Imphal and north to Kohima.

The command set-up in Burma as far as 14th Army was concerned was rather top heavy. The Supreme Commander, Lord Louis Mountbatten, gave his orders to General Giffard, commanding 11th Army Group, who commanded only one army, Lieutenant-General Slim's 14th Army. 14th Army initially had under command XV Corps (Lieutenant-General A.F.P. Christison) in the Arakan, IV Corps (Lieutenant-General G.A.P. Scoones), the Northern Combat Area Command (Lieutenant-General J.W. Stilwell), and Special Force (Major-General O.C. Wingate). Later XXXIII Corps (Lieutenant-General M.G.N. Stopford) was formed in the Bramhaputra valley to counter the Japanese advance, and XV Corps came under the direct command of General Sir George Giffard's 11th Army Group.

Slim had previously underestimated the violence and momentum of Sakurai's attack in the Arakan, but the fly-in of

overwhelming numbers, coupled with his strict orders that all units should stand firm if their communications were cut and await supply by air, had converted what might have been a disaster in the Arakan to a morale-raising victory.

Slim realised from Intelligence reports that IV Corps might suffer similar long-range penetration attacks, but he thought that these could not be in a strength greater than two regiments. He made his plans accordingly. On the night of March 5-6 he allowed the Chindit airborne operation to start its fly-in across the Chindwin to block the Japanese communications facing General Stilwell's forces (N.C.A.C.), in accordance with the orders of the Combined Chiefs-of-Staff.

IV Corps consisted of three divisions (17th, 20th, and 23rd) and the 254th Indian Tank Brigade (with Shermans and Grants). The 17th Division, after its retreat from Burma in 1942, had stayed for two years patrolling in the 7,000-foot Tiddim Hills, 100 miles south of Imphal. This light division consisted of two, mainly Gurkha, brigades on a mule/jeep transport basis.

The 20th Division was based on Palel and Tamu south-east of Imphal and patrolled towards the Chindwin.

The 23rd Division (Major-General O.L. Roberts) was in reserve at Imphal.

Lieutenant-General Scoones, who had commanded IV Corps since its formation, was a clever, quiet, forceful personality who achieved results through efficiency and attention to detail rather than by flamboyant leadership. With him his subordinates would know that everything would be in its place and up to strength.

Scoone's plan, which had been approved by Slim, was, on being attacked, to withdraw his two forward divisions back to the wide open Imphal plain, where he would be able to bring to bear his superiority in tanks heavy artillery, and close air support, which could outgun and destroy anything that the Japanese could bring over the hills and across the Chindwin against them. He would then have three divisions, with a promise of a fourth to be flown in, to combat the Japanese raid. The vital factor in his plan was when to give the order for the 17th Division to start its 100-mile retirement back from Tiddim to Imphal.

Slim planned to fly in the 5th Indian Division (Major-General H.R. Briggs) from the Arakan as soon as news of an

attack in strength was confirmed. The 50th Parachute Brigade (Brigadier M.R.J. Hope-Thompson) was due to be flown into Imphal and directed towards Ukhrul. Scoones planned to fly out all unnecessary administrative personnel and the very large number of engineers and their civilian working force who were engaged on improving communications and airfields within the Imphal area. In fact over 40,000 "unwanted mouths" were flown out as the battle progressed.

IV Corps consisted eventually of the 5th, 17th, 20th, and 23rd Indian Divisions, the 50th Indian Parachute Brigade, and the 254th Indian Tank Brigade (Shermans and Grants), comprising 49 infantry battalions (nine British, 24 Indian, and 16 Gurkha), and 120 tanks. Besides this, IV Corps had the 8th Medium Regiment, Royal Artillery, with 5.5-inch guns, as well as the usual complement of divisional artillery and engineers. In all there were about 120,000 men, excluding constructional engineers and Royal Air Force.

The strength of the Japanese 15th Army which crossed the Chindwin was 84,280 Japanese and 7,000 Indians. A further 4,000 reinforcements arrived during operations. The Japanese divided each division into three columns of varying size and composition, according to their tasks, but the total number of units which can be compared with those of IV Corps were as follows: nine infantry regiments, totalling 26 battalions (one battalion of the 15th Division had been sent back to deal with the landing of the airborne forces, but was later returned to the 15th Division during its attack on Imphal); two heavy artillery regiments; and one tank regiment.

Besides these there were divisional artillery, with much of it on a light mountain pack basis, and three engineer regiments, which were often used as infantry.

The British XXXIII Corps at its maximum strength consisted of two divisions (British 2nd and 7th Indian, under Major-Generals J.M.L. Grover and F.W. Messervy respectively), the 149th Regiment, Royal Armoured Corps, the 23rd (L.R.P.) Brigade (Brigadier L.E.C.M. Perowne), the 3rd Special Service (Commando) Brigade (Brigadier W.I. Nonweiler), and the Lushai Brigade (Brigadier P.C. Marindin), totalling about 75,000 troops, including 34 infantry battalions (20 British, 11 Indian, and three Gurkha).

Yanagida started his advance to attack

Previous page: *Gurkha advance.*
△ *The District Commissioner's Bungalow, destroyed in the heavy fighting for Kohima.*

on the night of March 7-8. The 215th Regiment went up the high mountains to Fort White and crossed the Manipur river to get into a position west of the 17th Indian Division's position at Tiddim and Tongzang.

The 214th Regiment marched north-west and advanced directly on Tongzang. Both regiments formed blocks across the Tiddim–Imphal road. Cowan, commanding the 17th Indian Division, had not told his brigadiers that there were plans for withdrawal, so on March 13, when he got Scoones's order to withdraw, his brigades had to have time to see that the orders reached every man. This meant a 24-hour delay. This particular division, consisting of a preponderance of Gurkhas, was well trained and had great confidence in itself and its quiet commander. Withdrawal continued according to plan and at each road-block the Gurkhas put into operation plans they had rehearsed and the Japanese blocks were removed without great difficulty, but with considerable loss to the Japanese.

However, Scoones was apprehensive of how successfully the 17th Division would be able to carry out this 100-mile long withdrawal on a road through high hills and where there were ambush positions every few hundred yards. So he committed some of his reserve division, the 23rd, which he had moved to Torbung. The 37th and 49th Brigades, with a squadron of tanks, were moved forward to Milestone 100.

Yanagida pressed on, but his troops were losing their momentum and after the fourth block across the road had been successfully removed by the British forces, Yanagida became depressed. On the night of March 23, after receiving many casualties, Yanagida sent a rather panicky signal to Mutaguchi implying that his position was hopeless. Yanagida had been appalled at the success of the Sherman and Grant medium tanks, against which neither his artillery nor his anti-tank guns seemed to have any affect.

After an exchange of furious signals Mutaguchi decided to remove Yanagida

Moving further north, Yamauchi's 15th Division crossed the Chindwin on the night of March 15-16 and moved quickly up the hills towards Ukhrul. According to plan he also sent a detachment to make contact with Yamamoto's column on the Palel Road. By March 21 Yamamoto was in contact with the 50th Parachute Brigade at Ukhrul, where it had taken over from the 23rd Division's 49th Brigade, which in turn had been moved to assist the 17th Division. All this time it must be remembered that Mutaguchi was in Maymyo, 200 miles to the east, the pleasant

▽ *The Tennis Court area just west of the District Commissioner's Bungalow, also destroyed in the short, savage fight for Kohima.*

and sent for a successor. It must be emphasised that this took place at the beginning of the campaign and affected the command and consequently the morale of the division on which the success of the whole operation depended.

Major-General Yamamoto's column which, it will be remembered, had the preponderance of Japanese armour, advanced quickly and surely up the Kabaw valley until by March 11 it had reached a position at Maw on the right flank of Gracey's 20th Indian Division. Gracey had taken his brigade commanders into his confidence about what action the division would take when Scoones gave the order to withdraw. So his brigades knew exactly what to do when he ordered them to destroy unnecessary stores, disengage, move back, and reform on the Shenam Heights just east of Palel. This withdrawal took place in good order and without a hitch, but was followed up by Yamamoto. Heavy fighting soon took place on the Palel road at a point that became known as Nippon Hill.

The Japanese Mitsubishi Ki-46-II "Dinah" reconnaissance aircraft

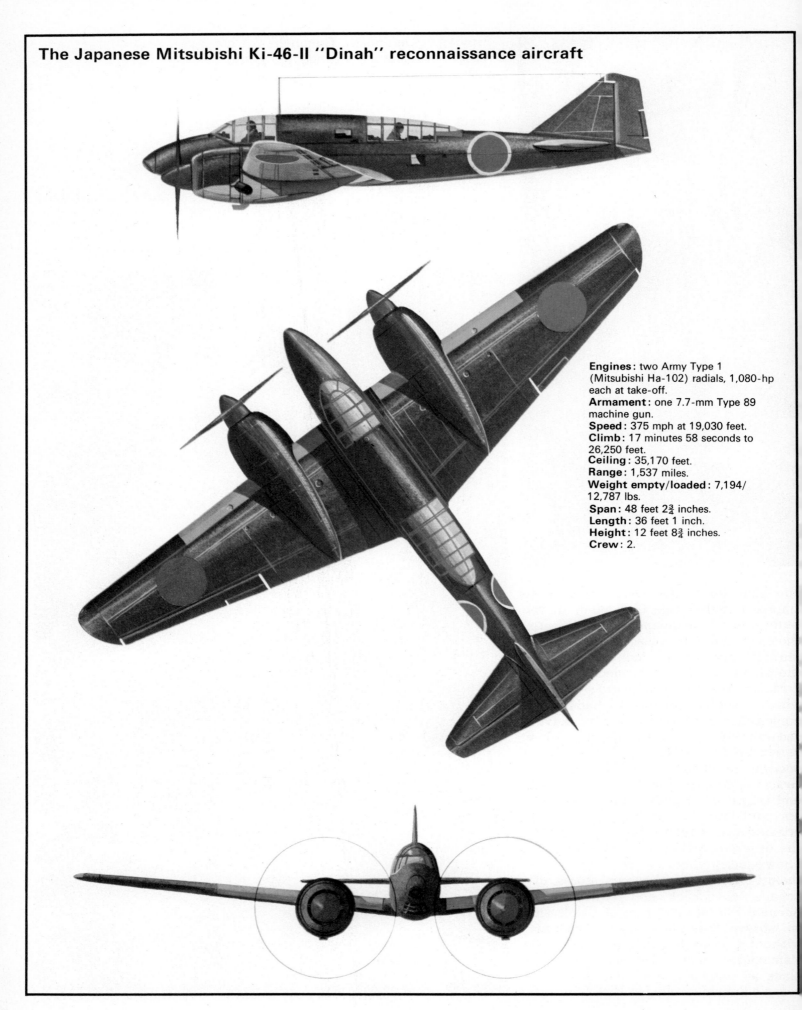

Engines: two Army Type 1 (Mitsubishi Ha-102) radials, 1,080-hp each at take-off.
Armament: one 7.7-mm Type 89 machine gun.
Speed: 375 mph at 19,030 feet.
Climb: 17 minutes 58 seconds to 26,250 feet.
Ceiling: 35,170 feet.
Range: 1,537 miles.
Weight empty/loaded: 7,194/12,787 lbs.
Span: 48 feet 2$\frac{3}{4}$ inches.
Length: 36 feet 1 inch.
Height: 12 feet 8$\frac{3}{4}$ inches.
Crew: 2.

ill station in which he had set up his headquarters. It was from this viewpoint that he sent signals exhorting his three divisional commanders to greater effort.

The 15th Division's orders were to by-pass Ukhrul and move towards the hills north of the Imphal plain to seize Kangla-ongbi.

Further north still, Sato's 31st Division which, having been in the area for many months, had had time to reconnoitre the routes over the hills, and done remark-bly well. Crossing the Chindwin bet-ween Homalin and Tamanthi on the night of March 15-16, his left-hand column reached Ukhrul, where it made contact with Yamauchi's forces. Whilst Yama-uchi pushed on, Sato's left-hand column, under the command of Major-General Shigesburo Miyazaki, made contact with the Indian Parachute Brigade at Sang-hak near Ukhrul. After pushing out the paratroops, Miyazaki advanced north-west and set up a road block at Maram on March 27, a few miles south of Kohima.

Meanwhile Sato's 58th and 124th Regi-ments advanced on Jessami. Jessami was weakly held by the Assam Regiment and was captured on April 1.

Kohima itself had originally been de-fended by Brigadier D.F.W. Warren's 161st Brigade of the 5th Division, which had been flown up from the Arakan to Dimapur. When Lieutenant-General Stop-ford took command of the area with his

XXXIII Corps, he unfortunately withdrew Brigadier Warren from Kohima to protect Dimapur itself, where there were 60,000 unarmed rear echelon troops looking after the stores and administration. This move left Kohima virtually unprotected. Sato continued his advance and by April 15 Kohima itself was invested.

Meanwhile Giffard, commanding the 11th Army Group, had started to move the remainder of the 5th Indian Division from the Arakan into the Imphal plain, and had also given Slim orders that the 7th Indian Division should disengage in the Arakan and be available to be flown up to the Brahmaputra valley to join Stopford's XXXIII Corps. Two brigades of the 5th Indian Division were quickly flown into Imphal between March 19 and 29, whilst all unnecessary troops were in turn flown out.

Scoones had mapped out a very sensible defence of the Imphal plain. He formed fortresses or "boxes" around each area where there were stores or airfields, and had detailed a commander with staff in charge of that area with a force to defend it. This worked well, but when pressure from the Japanese intensified he had to reduce the size of these areas and give up some of the stores, which then fell into Japanese hands. By this time he had four divisions and the parachute brigade with the formidable 254th Medium Tank Brigade to fight his battle. He also had

2926

SEAC NEWSPAPER OFFICE

◁◁ *Men of the 5th Indian Division (Major-General H.R. Briggs) take the 8,000-foot Kennedy Peak on the Tiddim–Fort White road as the British push south from Imphal.*
△ *Keeping the troops informed –the S.E.A.C. newspaper office in Manipur.*
◁ *Brigadier P.C. Marindin, commander of the Lushai Brigade, congratulates his men on having killed 160 Japanese for the loss of only one of their own men in a recent engagement. The brigade, consisting of three regular battalions together with detachments of the Assam Rifles and Chin Levies, was formed on March 26 to guard the approaches to the Surma valley through the Lushai and Chin hills.*

△ *Garrison Hill, near the Tennis Court area in Kohima. After heavy fighting between May 4 and 7, the 6th and 33rd Brigades failed in their efforts to break past this point, and it was not until another major attack between the 11th and the 13th that the line of hills from the District Commissioner's Bungalow to Jail Hill was taken from the Japanese.*

27 squadrons of fighters and fighter-bombers at short call to harass and destroy the Japanese, who were better targets now that they were emerging into the open plain. It must also be remembered that on the high ground the hills were bare and Sato's 31st Division suffered heavily from air attack when caught out in the open at Litan during its advance on Kohima.

In the Brahmaputra valley XXXIII Corps, whose nucleus was the 2nd British Division (which had originally been the theatre reserve and had been training for operations in Sumatra or Malaya), was now forming fast. The 2nd Division had too many vehicles for the type of country, but as it advanced it soon learnt how to fight with only one road as its main axis. Stopford, realising his mistake in withdrawing Warren's 161st Brigade, sent them back to the Kohima area, where a tiny garrison of the Royal West Kents and Assam Rifles was holding out gallantly.

It was now five weeks since Sato had crossed the Chindwin, and his supplies were beginning to dry up. As far as his division was concerned, a disaster had occurred when the Chindits had cut his communications back to the railway at Indaw and had blown bridges behind ten transport companies (300 trucks) which were unable to get back from Homalin.

Sato signalled Mutaguchi that he was running out of supplies and was having to eat his mules. He suggested that he should start retiring whilst he still had some pack animals left. Mutaguchi was appalled by this message and sent some extremely rude signals to the conscientious Sato.

Meanwhile, the Chindit 23rd (L.R.P.) Brigade had been put under Stopford's command. He gave it the task of making a wide sweep to the east to get behind the Japanese 31st Division and to advance all the way to Ukhrul. The eight columns of the brigade pushed on along the footpaths over the high ridge with their mule transport and with supply by air. Many small actions were fought and although it was not possible in this country with its many paths to "cut" communications, the force threatened Sato's communications to such an extent that he told Mutaguchi that he must withdraw.

Mutaguchi was going through a bad time. He had replaced Yanagida with Major-General N. Tanaka, who was a tough, resilient, earthy soldier who had fought in north China. Mutaguchi had no luck with the 15th Division either, as the divisional commander, Yamauchi, died of malaria. He was replaced by Lieutenant-General U. Shibata, a man, it was said, "with an ox-like presence".

Mutaguchi was issuing orders of the day appealing to all ranks, saying that the throne of the Emperor depended on them and so on. But this did not move the intelligent and worldly-wise Sato. Muta-

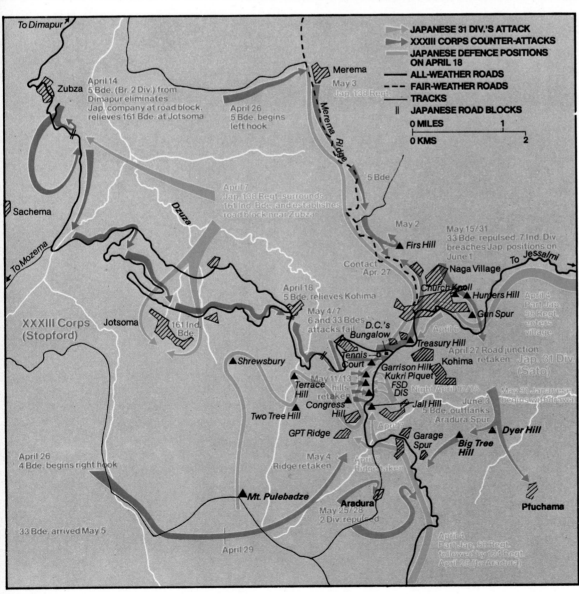

JAPANESE 31 DIV.'S ATTACK
XXXIII CORPS COUNTER-ATTACKS
JAPANESE DEFENCE POSITIONS
ON APRIL 18
—— ALL-WEATHER ROADS
- - - FAIR-WEATHER ROADS
—— TRACKS
‖ JAPANESE ROAD BLOCKS

0 MILES   1
0 KMS   2

To Dimapur

Zubza

April 14
5 Bde. (Br. 2 Div.) from
Dimapur eliminates
Jap. company at road block,
relieves 161 Bde. at Jotsoma.

Merema
May 3
Jap. 138 Regt.

April 26
5 Bde. begins
left hook

Merema Ridge

Sachema

April 7
Jap. 138 Regt. surrounds
161 Ind. Bde. and establishes
road block near Zubza

Dzuza

5 Bde.

May 2

▲ Firs Hill

To Mozema

Contact
Apr. 27

May 15/31
33 Bde. repulsed. 7 Ind. Div.
breaches Jap. positions on
June 1

To Jessalmi

▲ Naga Village

Church Knoll

▲ Hunters Hill

April 4
Part Jap.
58 Regt.
enters
village

April 18
5 Bde. relieves Kohima

XXXIII Corps
(Stopford)

Jotsoma

161 Ind.
Bde.

May 4/7
6 and 33 Bdes.
attacks fail

D.C.'s
Bungalow

▲ Shrewsbury

Tennis
Court

▲ Gun Spur

Treasury Hill

Kohima

April 6

April 27 Road junction
retaken

Jap. 31 Div.
(Sato)

May 11/13
hills
retaken

Garrison Hill
Kukri Piquet
FSD
DIS

Terrace
Hill

▲ Congress
Hill

Two Tree Hill

Night April 17/18

Jail Hill

May 31 Japanese
begins withdrawal

GPT Ridge

June 3
5 Bde. outflanks
Aradura Spur

▲ Dyer Hill

April 26
4 Bde. begins right hook

May 4
Ridge retaken

April
Ridge taken

Garage
Spur

Big Tree
Hill

▲ Mt. Pulebadze

Aradura

May 25/28
2 Div. repulsed

Pfuchama

33 Bde. arrived May 5

April 29

April 4
Part Jap. 58 Regt.
followed by 124 Regt.
April 26 (to Aradura)

△ Men of the 3/10th Gurkha
Rifles (23rd Indian Division) on
Scraggy Hill, a point dominating
the Palel–Tamu road south-east
of Imphal. The hill was taken
on July 24 at the cost of 112
Gurkha casualties.
◁ The desperate battle for the
little town of Kohima.

◁ *Two Japanese tanks knocked out by Rifleman Ganju Lama of the 1/7th Gurkha Rifles. This action, part of the 17th Indian Division's struggle around Bishenpur against the Japanese 33rd Division, won Lama the V.C.*
▷ *The Garrison Hill battlefield at Kohima.*
▽ *Gurkhas clear up Scraggy after the short, sharp action that won it for the British.*

△ Lieutenant-General G.A.P. Scoones, commander of IV Corps in the Imphal–Kohima area.

guchi sent staff officers to see him, but Sato took no notice of them. On April 30 Sato signalled again, pointing out the hopelessness of his position. These signals continued until on June 1 Sato signalled "Propose retreating from Kohima with rearguard." Mutaguchi replied "Retreat and I will court-marshal you." Sato replied "Do as you please I will bring you down with me." This gives some idea of the division and state of mind of the Japanese force commanders, who were fighting against odds at Kohima and Imphal. Sato was quite adamant as he saw his men staggering back half naked, without ammunition and weapons, and relying on bamboo shoots and roots for their sustenance. He was determined that Mutaguchi should be brought back to Tokyo for court-marshal for basic neglect of administration.

Sato left Miyazaki with 750 of his best and fittest men to form a rearguard south of Kohima, which had now been cleared by the 2nd Division, and retreated. The rest of his division, all supplies having been stopped by the Chindits, ceased to exist and melted away.

Around Imphal, however, very heavy fighting continued. With their two new divisional commanders, the 15th Division and 33rd Divisions were attacking Scoones from all directions, and it was only as a result of the skill and high morale of his divisions, coupled with the technical superiority of his tanks, the R.A.F., and the 8th Medium Artillery Regiment, that he could keep at bay the fanatical assaults of these Japanese.

It is worth digressing here to point out that defence against well-trained soldiers who are quite prepared to take part in suicidal attacks is quite different from defence against reasonable men who, when they see a situation is hopeless, will withdraw or surrender. This was one reason why commanders who came from

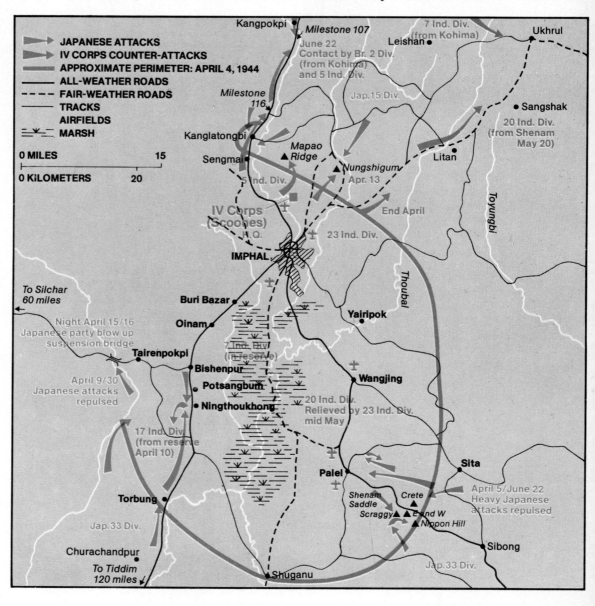

the European theatre took some time to settle down to the new type of tactics. Their enemy in this theatre had not only to be outmanoeuvred, beaten, and have their weapons overcome, but they themselves had to be destroyed one by one.

From a distance, in London and Washington, it appeared that IV Corps was not making sufficient effort to fight its way out, and some criticism was received on this count, but IV Corps had also to expend and disperse men to protect airfields and stores against suicide attacks and so was not quite free to launch the strong offensive towards Ukhrul which it had been ordered to make. Both the 20th and 23rd Divisions had been ordered to capture Ukhrul, but both had made little progress.

The 2nd Division continued its advance down the road and on June 22 contact was made between the two corps at Milestone 109, just north of the Imphal plain. Stopford had advanced 70 miles

from Kohima but Scoones had fought less than ten miles uphill out of the plain. The monsoon was now in full spate, but Slim ordered the two corps to pursue. This was easier said than done. The Japanese 15th Division, suffering severely from disease and lack of supplies, as the Chindits had cut their communications east to the railway, was in a very bad way. But it managed to hold out at Ukhrul and had prevented the pincer movement which Slim had designed to cut it off.

The 33rd Division, with its new commander, was in better shape and was fighting well on the roads running south to Kalemyo and Kalewa.

The 19th Indian Division had joined the British 2nd Division in its advance south so that the Allied forces had managed to collect the equivalent of nine divisions with overwhelming air superiority against the Japanese three divisions and the I.N.A. brigade. As the monsoon wore on, the Japanese defeat became more com-

△ *Troops wait on a forward airfield in the Imphal hills before going into action. One of the most noteworthy features of the campaign was the way in which Allied air superiority allowed supplies and reinforcements to be flown in.*

2934

plete as a result of disease and lack of supplies. The British have the reputation of not being good in pursuit, and there was undoubtedly a slackening in follow-up, but the British commanders felt that the monsoon was completing their victory. Chandra Bhose's I.N.A. melted away, whilst Sato returned accusing Mutaguchi of negligence and incompetence, stating that his division had received no ammunition or supplies for six weeks. Mutaguchi had on May 15 moved his headquarters to Tamu, and it was only then when he saw the condition of his men and experienced the absolute dominance of the air by the R.A.F. that he realised the extent to which he was being defeated. Of the 88,000 Japanese (including reinforcements) who had crossed the Irrawaddy, 53,505 became casualties, including 30,502 killed, missing, or dead of disease.

Victory at Kohima/Imphal would probably not have been possible without absolute air superiority, air supply, and close air support.

Deliveries to IV Corps on the Imphal plain between April 18 and June 30 totalled 18,824 tons of stores of all sorts and at least 12,561 personnel. On their return flights the transport aircraft (R.A.F. and U.S.A.A.F.) evacuated 13,000 casualties and 43,000 non-combatants. The total number of reinforcements carried is difficult to calculate, as space was always made available to take in extra men. But 1,540 sorties were flown to move the 5th Division, the 7th Division (33rd and 89th Brigades), and the 4th Brigade of the 2nd Division to the Central Front. The Lushai Brigade and the 23rd Brigade were wholly, and XXXIII Corps was partially, supplied by air during their advance.

Between March 10 and July 30, R.A.F. fighters of the 3rd T.A.F. flew 18,860 sorties and those of the U.S.A.A.F. 10,800 sorties, losing 130 R.A.F. and 40 U.S. A.A.F. aircraft. The majority of these 29,660 sorties flown was for close air support of troops on the ground. During the same period the J.A.A.F. flew 1,750 sorties.

This gives some idea of the Allied dominance of the air and the importance of the construction of all-weather airfields on the ground in this campaign.

In spite of their evident superiority in numbers, all ranks of the British and Indian units had fought hard and very well, and had learnt to trust each other.

◁ *A Japanese fox-hole in the Kohima area, now in Allied hands.*
△ *Private Reg Maycox* (left), *a member of a small patrol being briefed by its company commander* (with pipe).

▽ Kohima after the battle.
▽ ▽ Naga hill people inspect equipment abandoned by the Japanese as they were forced off Garrison Hill.
▽ ▷ Mules are ferried across the swift Manipur river on special rafts, which prevent the mules seeing the water and panicking.

British and Indian casualties during the battles of Imphal and Kohima were just under 16,700, of which approximately a quarter were incurred at Kohima. In spite of strict medical and anti-malarial precautions, sickness caused more than 12 times the number of battle casualties, although many of those who went sick could return to their units.

After Imphal was relieved on June 22, Slim reformed his forces on that front. IV Corps, with the 17th and 20th Divisions who had been holding the line for two years, was withdrawn to India for a refit. The 50th Parachute Brigade was also withdrawn. Slim moved his own headquarters into Imphal and ordered Stopford's XXXIII Corps to continue the pursuit of the Japanese 33rd Division southwards. XXXIII Corps now consisted of the British 2nd, 5th and 20th Indian, and 11th East African Divisions. Movement through the mountains in the monsoon, coupled with extensive demolitions by the Japanese 33rd Division, slowed the British advance to a snail's pace, so that the Chindwin was not reached or crossed until early December, by which time Northern Combat Area Command's British 36th Division (Festing) had advanced down the railway from Mogaung to within 100 miles north of Mandalay. This "turned" the front of the Japanese facing XXXIII Corps so that the former swung back facing north, with their axis on Kalewa.

The Japanese 15th Army had been beaten. The Allies were now on the dry plains of Burma where tanks, artillery, and aircraft could be used to the maximum effect. The time was ripe for the ejection of the Japanese from Burma. The orders given to the Supreme Commander, Lord Louis Mountbatten, by the Chiefs-of-Staff had been fulfilled. He now received new orders to drive the Japanese out of Burma completely, by advancing on Mandalay and then on Rangoon.

1944

January

29. Preliminary three day bombardment of Kwajalein atoll by Task Force 58.

February

1. U.S. 7th Infantry Division and 4th Marine Division land on Kwajalein, Roi, and Namur.

4. Japanese 55th Division counterattacks in Arakan.

5. Americans mop up on Kwajalein. Chindit 16th Brigade begins move to Indaw.

7. Allied force cut off in "Admin. Box" on the Arakan front. Kwajalein atoll secured; U.S. losses 372 dead and 1,000 wounded, Japanese 7,870 killed out of garrison of 8,000.

11. Supplies air dropped to "Admin. Box".

12. Allies occupy Rooke Island and Gorissi in New Britain.

13. Allied forces begin counterattack in Arakan.

15. New Zealand troops seize Green Island.

17. Beginning of two-day air attack on Japanese naval and air base at Truk. Japanese lose 200,000 tons of shipping and 275 aircraft. U.S. 22nd Marines land on Engebi Island in Eniwetok atoll.

21. Tojo becomes Chief of the Japanese Army General Staff. Eniwetok secured; U.S. losses 339 dead.

23. U.S. Task Force 58 attacks shipping and aircraft in the Marianas.

25. British clear Japanese from Ngakyedyauk Pass in Burma. 7th Indian Division's "Admin. Box" relieved.

27. Allied air attacks against Momote and Lorengau in the Admiralties and targets in New Guinea in preparation for invasion of Los Negros in the Admiralties.

29. U.S. 1st Cavalry Division lands on Los Negros island in the Admiralty Islands.

March

1. General Swift is ordered to develop air and naval facilities on Los Negros. Chindit 16th Brigade crosses the Chindwin.

4. U.S. and Chinese forces make pincer movement against Japanese in Hukawng Valley.

5. Chindits land at Broadway and Chowringee.

6. U.S. Marines land on Talasea on New Britain.

11. Indians take Buthidaung on Arakan front.

12. U.S. Marines occupy Wotho atoll. Razabil taken on the Arakan front.

13. British and West African troops land on the Arakan coast.

14. British withdraw from Tiddim to the Imphal plain.

16. Japanese cross the Chindwin river to cut the Kohima-Imphal road.

17. White City blocking position set up at Mawlu by Chindits. British demolish Manipur bridge in Kohima-Imphal region.

20. U.S. Marines land on Emerau Island in the Bismarcks.

22. Japanese reach point 30 miles east of Imphal.

24. Counter-offensive in Bougainville.

25. Death of Wingate in air crash.

26. Attack on Indaw fails. British troops retreat to Imphal after delaying the Japanese advance.

27. Major-General W.D.A. Lentaigne succeeds Wingate.

29. Siege of Imphal begins. U.S. Task Force 58 begins three day attack on targets in the Carolines. Imphal-Kohima road cut.

April

4. Japanese begin attack on Kohima.

11. Japanese abandon Gasmata, Cape Hoskins.

13. Australians enter Bogadjim.

19. British troops from Dimapur link up with besieged Kohima.

22. Landings at Hollandia and Aitape by U.S. forces supported by the 7th Fleet.

24. U.S. War Department announces that only invasion of Japan will ensure its collapse. Aitape declared secure; U.S. losses 450 dead, Japanese 9,000.

27. U.S. land-based fighters operate from Aitape in support of Hollandia forces.

28. Japanese advance in Honan Province. U.S. and Chinese troops move up Mogaung valley toward Myitkyina.

29. U.S. Task Force 58 begins two-day strike on Truk atoll.

May

3. Allies take high ground above Maungdaw-Buthidaung road, Arakan.

5. 14th Army begins attack on Assam. Japanese announce that Admiral Koga was killed in March.

8. Japanese attack 14th Army in Manipur hills.

9. Japanese capture Lushan and cut the last sector of the Peking-Hangkow railway.

16. Kohima ridge cleared of last Japanese troops.

17. Wakde and Insoemanai islands captured by U.S. forces. Myitkyina airfield captured by Allies.

19. Merrill's U.S. and Chinese troops partially encircle Myitkyina.

20. U.S. 5th Fleet aircraft begin two day attack on Marcus Island.

23. Chinese begin counter-offensive on Honan front and capture Chefang on the Burma Road.

25. Chindits withdraw after Blackpool stronghold is overrun.

27. U.S. 41st Division encounters light opposition in the early stages of its landing on Biak island. MacArthur announces the strategic end of the New Guinea campaign. Monsoons restrict Burma operations.

29. First tank battle of S.W. Pacific is fought on Biak.

June

2. Chinese besiege Myitkyina.

3. End of the battle of Kohima.

7. Americans capture Mokmer airfield on Biak.

11. U.S. Task Force 58 begins bombardment of and fighter operations off Marianas.

15. U.S. 2nd and 4th Marine Divisions land on Saipan against strong opposition. Navy aircraft attack Bonins and Iwo Jima.

16. Fierce Japanese counter-attacks on Saipan repulsed. U.S.A.A.F. raids Japan from Chinese mainland bases.

18. Marines take Aslito airfield on

Saipan.

19. Battle of the Philippine Sea. Japanese lose 346 aircraft in "Great Marianas Turkey Shoot", and two fleet carriers.

22. 14th Army clears Kohima-Imphal road and relieves Imphal. Chindits begin attack on Mogaung.

26. Mogaung taken.

July

4. Marines take Garapan and Flores Point on Saipan.

7. Admiral Nagumo and General Saito commit suicide on Saipan.

9. 3,000 Japanese in final counter-attack on Saipan. Total losses, Japanese 27,000 killed, U.S. 3,116. Ghandi concedes Muslim's right to be separate from Hindu India.

10. Japanese cleared from Ukhrul area in Burma. Japanese counter-attack near Aitape in New Guinea.

18. Japanese begin retreat from Kohima-Imphal area. Tojo cabinet resigns; Tojo replaced as Army chief by Umezu.

21. U.S. Marines and Army land on Guam.

22. American forces repel counter-attacks on Guam.

25. U.S. 2nd and 4th Marine Divisions land on Tinian. Heavy fighting on Guam.

26. Roosevelt arrives in Honolulu to meet MacArthur and Nimitz. Heavy fighting continues on Guam.

30. U.S. troops land on Vogelkop peninsula in New Guinea.

31. Fierce fighting near Aitape. U.S. troops move by sea to Cape Sansapor.

August

2. Tinian secured at a loss of 389 U.S. killed.

3. Chinese capture Myitkyina.

10. Guam secured; 10,000 Japanese killed, U.S. losses over 1,400.

27. Last Chindits evacuated to India.

29. Allies capture Pinbaw in Burma.

31. U.S. task force begins attacks on Bonins, West Carolines, and Visayas archipelago.

September

3. U.S. Navy bomb and shell targets in Marianas, Caroline, and Volcano islands.

5. Japanese forces destroyed at Bhamo and Tengyuel in Burma.

9. Ghandi and Jinnah meet to discuss Pakistan.

10. U.S. 3rd Fleet begins two day strike against the Palaus.

13. U.S. Marines land on Peleliu in Palaus, Army at Morotai. Chinese capture Teng-chung.

17. U.S. Army assaults and captures Angaur in three-day battle.

21. U.S. Navy aircraft attack ships and aircraft in Manila area.

22. U.S. forces land on Ulithi atoll.

24. Japanese counter-attack on Peleliu.

25. Chiang Kai-shek refuses to accept Stilwell as commander of Chinese forces.

October

9. U.S. 3rd Fleet bombards Marcus Island. Nimitz decides to invade Iwo Jima in the Volcano-Bonins.

10. The 3rd Fleet attacks airfields and shipping around Okinawa.

13-16. Battle off Formosa: Japanese lose more than 650 aircraft and sustain damage to their shore instalations.

17. U.S. Rangers land on islands in approaches to Leyte Gulf. Stilwell ordered home to Washington.

20. X Corps of the U.S. 6th Army begins landings on Leyte on two beach heads.

21. Japanese counter-attack on Leyte.

22. American 6th Army mops up at Tacloban on Leyte.

23-24. Battle of the Sibuyan Sea. Japanese battleship *Musashi* and U.S. Navy carrier *Princeton* sunk.

24-25. The Battle of Surigao Strait. Vice-Admiral Shoji Nishumura goes down with flagship *Yamashiro*.

26. Leyte Gulf battle ends. Japanese losses 4 carriers, 3 battleships, 6 heavy and 4 light cruisers, 11 destroyers, and a submarine. U.S. losses 1 light carrier, 2 escort carriers, 2 destroyers, 1 destroyer escort.

27. *Kamikaze* attacks on Task Force 38 in Philippines.

November

2. 14th Army takes Mawlu in Burma.

7. Victor Sorge executed in Japan.

10. Japanese capture U.S. air base at Kweilin in Kwangsi Province.

11. U.S. Navy bombards Iwo Jima.

16. 14th Army captures Kalemyo, cutting Japanese communications with the south.

24. B-29's raid Tokyo from bases in the Marianas for the first time.

25. *Kamikaze* attacks on U.S. Navy in Leyte Gulf and near Luzon.

December

1. 14th Army reaches Pinwe.

8. U.S.A.A.F. begins 72-day assault on Iwo Jima.

10. 14th Army reaches Indaw.

15. Western Visayan Task Force lands on Mindoro, begins airfield construction. Chinese take Bhamo in Burma. 14th Army takes Indaw.

25. Organised resistance ceases on Leyte.

28. Mindoro airfield operational.

30. 14th Army takes Kaduma.

1945

January

1. U.S. 8th Army begins four month mopping up operations on Leyte.

4. Japanese conventional and *kamikaze* aircraft attack invasion convoys approaching Lingayen Gulf.

6. U.S. Fleet reaches Lingayen Gulf under heavy aerial attack.

7. 14th Army reaches Shwebo.

9. U.S. 6th Army lands at Lingayen Gulf on Luzon Island.

10. U.S. 6th Army gains ground, Gangaw taken.

14. British 19th Div. crosses the Irrawaddy at Kyaukmyaung.

15. Japanese launch offensive for Suichwan airfields. Task Force 38 attacks Formosa and China coast airfields and shipping.

21. 14th Army enters Monywa.

22. Burma Road reopened.

24. U.S. 14th Air Force abandons Suichon air base. British seaborne landing in Gulf of Bengal.

25. Americans capture Clark Field on Luzon.

28. Supplies reach China over the Burma Ledo Road.

February

4. U.S. troops enter the outskirts of

Manila.

5. MacArthur orders Japanese in north Luzon to be contained; attack concentrated against Manila. Australians land on New Britain.

16. Pre-invasion bombardment of Iwo Jima. Indian brigade lands on Arakan. U.S. paratroops land on Corregidor.

17. Americans occupy Bataan peninsula. British hold Shweli bridgehead against Japanese counterattack. Task Force 58 raids Tokyo. 170 frogmen lost on reconnaissance of Iwo Jima beach defences.

19. U.S. 4th and 5th Marine Divisions land on Iwo Jima, suffering 2,420 casualties in first day.

20. Marines capture Airfield Number 1 on Iwo Jima, and move towards Mt. Suribachi.

23. Suribachi stormed, and American flag raised on the crest.

24. Manila occupied; some Japanese remain in isolated pockets.

27. Americans land on Verde island off Manila.

28. Corregidor declared secure.

March

3. Manila Bay cleared and Manila secured.

4. First B-29's land on Iwo Jima. Meiktila in Burma taken.

8. U.S. troops land at Samboanga on Mindanao.

10. B-29 raid on Tokyo destroys $16\frac{1}{2}$ acres. French and Japanese troops fight in Hanoi.

13. 14th Army captures Maymyo, cutting Japanese escape route from Mandalay.

14. Marines mop up pockets of resistance on Iwo Jima and strike north.

15. Indian 17th Div. besieged in Meiktila. U.S. 6th Army squeezes out Japanese on Luzon.

16. Organised resistance ends on Iwo Jima.

17. 14th Army takes Sagain and Ava. Final mopping up on Iwo Jima.

19. Task Force 58 attacks Japanese naval units in Kure-Kobe area, fighters strafe airfields. Japanese evacuate Mandalay.

20. Nagoya hit by fire raid by B-29's.

26. Last Japanese on Iwo Jima make suicide attack. Total losses in Iwo Jima campaign U.S. 6,891 killed,

Japanese over 21,000.

27. Royal Navy Task Force 57 bombards Sakishima Island.

29. Okinawa shelled and bombed by U.S. Navy.

April

1. Landings on Okinawa. After a heavy bombardment 60,000 troops establish a beach-head.

3. MacArthur appointed C.-in-C., U.S. Armed Forces, Pacific; Admiral Nimitz Pacific naval commander.

4. Increased Japanese resistance on Okinawa.

7. U.S. fleet off Okinawa attacked by conventional and *kamikaze* aircraft; 383 shot down, six U.S. ships sunk and 24 damaged. *Yamato* sunk on *kamikaze* mission, 2,488 men lost.

12. Death of President Roosevelt.

13. Chinese launch new attacks on Honan and Hupeh.

16. U.S. 6th Army on Luzon clears San Francisco area. 14th Army takes Taungup.

17. Americans make further landings on Mindanao at Malabang and Cotabato.

22. Indians capture Burmese oilfields at Yenangyaung.

23. U.S. 8th Army ends central Philippines campaign by capturing Cebu.

30. Hitler commits suicide in Berlin. 14th Army captures Pegu. Five days of *kamikaze* strikes sink 20 and damage 157 U.S. and Allied ships at Okinawa.

May

1. Australians land on Tarakan island. British airborne troops land south of Rangoon.

2. Prome and Pegu in Burma captured.

3. Indian troops enter Rangoon.

4. *Kamikazes* sink 17 ships in 24 hours at Okinawa.

9. German surrender in Berlin is ratified.

10. 14th Army links up with troops from Arakan, cutting off western area of the Irrawaddy. U.S. Marines attack across Asa estuary on Okinawa.

11. U.S. 10th Army launches two-corps assault on Okinawa. Australians cross the Hongoria on Bougainville.

13. Australians occupy Wewak peninsula.

14. Australians occupy Wewak village and harbour.

15. U.S. Navy renews attacks on Mindanao.

16. Dutch forces make landing on Tarakan island.

18. Chinese occupy Foochow. U.S. Marines take Sugar Loaf on Okinawa.

19. Japanese resistance in Ipoh area of Luzon ends.

21. Americans capture supply base at Malaybalay on Mindanao. Japanese begin to withdraw from Shuri on Okinawa.

25. U.S. Joint Chiefs-of-Staff complete plan for Operation "Olympic"; Japanese mainland to be invaded November 1. 14th Army captures Bassein.

June

1. Japanese retreat on Luzon, Mindanao, and Okinawa. Chinese attack north of Foochow.

4. U.S. Marines land on North Oroku peninsula and advance rapidly.

5. Marines in Oroku seize Naha airfield.

8. U.S. 6th Army reaches the Magat on Luzon.

10. Australian 9th Division invades Borneo; Labuan airfield taken.

11. Australians land near Chabai.

13. Australians capture Brunei town. Resistance ends on Oroku peninsula.

15. Chinese advance in Kwangsi.

18. Organised resistance ends on Mindanao. Lt.-General Simon Bolivar Buckner killed on Okinawa. Australians reach Tutong in Borneo.

19. Australians land on northern end of Brunei Bay.

20. Australians land at Lutong on Sarawak. Burmese leaders confer in Rangoon.

22. A two-prong assault by the Army and Marines reduces the last organised resistance on Okinawa. Japanese losses 107,500 known dead with about 20,000 sealed in caves during fighting, 7,400 prisoners. U.S. Army losses 7,374, Navy 5,000 killed. 5th Fleet lost 36 vessels with 368 damaged. All now ready for invasion of Japan.